The 7 Mindsets

To Live Your Ultimate Life

The 7 Mindsets

To Live Your Ultimate Life

An unexpected blueprint
for an extraordinary life

Scott Shickler & Jeff Waller

Creators of the 7 Mindsets

*For every book purchased, a book will be donated to a student through the **Magic Wand Foundation**, a non-profit organization dedicated to empowering youth to live their dreams.*

Author photographs by Haigwood Studios Photography

Copyeditors: Alice M. Ormiston and Jadd Shickler
Contributing editor: Vincent Begley
Cover Design & Layout: Rand Cabus, Privateer Graphic Design and Marketing
Composition: Alice M. Ormiston

7 Mindsets Media is a division of 7 Mindsets, a division of Excent Corporation.

ISBN: 978-0-9847824-0-6

"A candle loses nothing by lighting another candle."

-Father James Keller

We dedicate this book to our children

Jaxson, Hayden, Daniel, Ana Lucia and Sienna
You make the world a brighter place.

It is also dedicated with love to

Grace and Lilly
Our blueprints for extraordinary wives

What people are saying about The 7 Mindsets to Live Your Ultimate Life:

"The 7 Mindsets book is fascinating and spot-on. It's a new "classic" in the company of *Think and Grow Rich* and *How to Win Friends and Influence People."*

Larry Hart
Group Chair at Vistage International, GA

"Throughout my career, I have had the opportunity to meet many successful people, and you can immediately tell they have determined mindsets that drive them non-stop towards their goals. Every parent and teacher should be sharing these 7 Mindsets with our children for them to flourish in this new highly competitive global marketplace."

Famous Dave Anderson, Founder
World's Best BBQ Joint and America's Best Tasting Ribs!

"Shickler and Waller have hit the bullseye. The 7 Mindsets are exactly what's needed to transform an ordinary life into an extraordinary one."

Dahlynn McKowen,
Coauthor, Chicken Soup for the Soul

"It is so powerful to observe the impact of the 7 Mindsets on students. It's like the veil that is covering the secret to success is lifted and they begin to realize that it is within their control to choose to embrace these seven mindsets, which will ultimately change the trajectory of their lives."

Amy Hodgson
Educator /Superintendent in Michigan

"The 7 Mindsets is one of the most phenomenal and revolutionary messages of our time. The theories have inspired a great upgrade in my thinking towards living an extraordinary life, and it is spreading very quickly among young people here in Africa, poised to bring a much needed generational shift."
Adeniyi Bankole
Lawyer/Social Entrepreneur, Nigeria

"The 7 Mindsets have been an important turning point in my life. Not only did I start thinking like a global citizen, but I have developed a passion to make the world a better place. I am now using them as a daily compass for my life and I highly recommend others do the same."
James Mwakichako
Student, Kenya

"I have seen firsthand how the 7 Mindsets have transformed students from around the world. Students are equipped with principles that help them take ownership of their lives, focus their time and energy, and positively impact the world around them. The world would be a better place if all students were taught the 7 Mindsets!"
Bill Schulte
Educator, FL

"If you want to transform your business, then every employee should read this book. The 7 Mindsets will raise the level of performance from everyone who puts them into action."
Susan Wilson Solovic
NY Times Best Selling Author & CEO, It's Your Biz

"No one is better suited to understand the trends and issues of today's teenagers than themselves. The research and message of *The 7 Mindsets* not only empower teenagers to take ownership of the challenges facing their generation; it also gives them tools to help them immediately take action. I have personally seen the insights of *The 7 Mindsets* put into action and it is nothing short of awesome."

Wesley Bender
Youth Leader – YMCA, GA

"Working with business professionals, I hear comments about the apathy of teens today. Through the mindsets, young adults are given a vehicle to put their energy and imagination to work. The results are absolutely incredible and may be exactly what we need to change the business community and the world."

April Farlow
Leadership Instructor/Consultant

"The 7 Mindsets were planted in my son's heart at the right time and have influenced him to pursue extraordinary achievements. From starting his own business when he was 13 to his current leadership positions at school, to pursuing his dreams in nuclear engineering; it all started by living the mindsets."

Manual Carvallo
Parent

Contents

Introduction

I don't know how many people in the world can look back and recognize the moment that changed their lives, but I'm lucky enough to be able to do so.

My life changed on the day I walked into a Boys and Girls Club in Newark, New Jersey.

It all started when I was asked to be a guest speaker one Saturday afternoon to a group of students. I had never been to Newark, and was actually a bit afraid. At that time, Newark was considered one of the most dangerous cities in the country. Not only was it number one in auto theft, it was the leader in the latest craze of carjacking.

So there I was, talking to a group of 10-year-olds about the only thing I felt confident speaking about: business. I wasn't a teacher. I was an entrepreneur fresh out of college. I wasn't even sure if 10-year-olds could comprehend the concept of business, let alone be interested in how businesses worked. Unsure of what to expect, I was introduced as a business owner, and my heart warmed when I saw a spark of interest in their eyes. Out of curiosity, I asked if any of them were interested in starting their own companies one day, or maybe even being their own bosses. Almost every hand went up, and I'm sure I had a startled look on my face. Then a student asked how he could become a business owner like me, and sort of leaned toward me in anticipation. I wasn't expecting this question, and, as I paused for a moment to try to respond in a way that made sense to a 10-year-old, the teacher standing in the back of the room chimed in.

The teacher told the students that, in order to start their own business, they needed to graduate from high school, go to college, get an MBA, write a business plan, and raise a lot of money. When they had done all that, they would have a three out of ten chance of success in a business of their own. In less than 30 seconds, that teacher had completely changed the energy in the room. I watched as the students lost their enthusiasm and many literally slumped down in their chairs. The strange thing was, I had heard this advice before... when I was a kid filled with curiosity. But having lived a different experience than the one the teacher was describing, I knew things not only could be different, but *should* be different. I told the kids that their teacher had indeed pointed out *one* way to become a business owner, but that I knew of another way for all of them to become their own boss much sooner—perhaps even in a matter of days or weeks. With that simple statement of hope, they all perked up again.

Over the next four weeks, I continued to volunteer. I took the students to a local wholesaler, giving them each ten dollars in seed capital so they could buy merchandise to start their business. I showed them how to make posters, flyers, and marketing materials. I encouraged them to come up with names for their businesses, give themselves titles, and I had business cards made up for each of them. We set up a market in the lobby of the Boys & Girls Club where the fledgling entrepreneurs sold their wares. Afterwards, I took them to a local bank and helped them open savings accounts to hold their newly earned money. Everything appeared to be going great, they seemed to be natural entrepreneurs... and then I got a call telling me the club director wanted to talk to me before I taught another class.

With some trepidation, I entered her office.

The Director said to me, "Mr. Shickler," and paused, which didn't sound like a good start to me. "I've been getting a lot of calls from parents about this new program we're offering and, interestingly, I didn't even know we had a new program."

I immediately said that it wasn't really a program, I was just trying to teach the students about business.

That's when she pointed to a ten-year-old boy playing outside her office and asked, "Do you see that kid over there? Last month he stole a car. The month before that, he stole two cars!"

I said, "You're kidding right? Jamal?" Jamal was one of the students in my business class. "He stole a car? But he's only ten years old. He can't even see over the steering wheel!" Flustered and not sure what to do, and almost fearing the answer to my question, I asked, "What has he done this month?"

"That's just it!" she said, "He hasn't done anything wrong all month! He seems really engaged in your program."

I was still a little unsure where things were headed. "Actually," I timidly interjected, "I don't really have a program."

The director smiled and said, "You do now."

My life changed that day, and (little did I know) I would spend the next two decades teaching entrepreneurship, financial literacy, and personal achievement to tens of thousands of students and educators across the country and around the world. I've written books, started several multi-million dollar education companies, and seen my work featured in an array of media from CNN, ABC and NBC News to *The Wall Street Journal* and the *New York Times*.

This book, however, is by far the most important piece of work I've ever done, together with my colleague and co-author, Jeff Waller. This book is the culmination of years of research and millions of dollars invested in search of the answer to a simple question: "If every kid wants to grow up to live a happy and successful life, why do so few achieve it?"

Every parent wants his or her child to grow up to be happy and successful. Every teacher wants the same for their students. Billions of dollars are spent each year on public and private schools, and by a myriad of non-profit organizations on one seemingly simple goal... preparing young people for a successful life. Unfortunately, however, for all the billions of dollars and hours spent, things are just not working. One doesn't have to look far to find the signs of failure. One out of three students who enter first grade will not graduate from high school. One in five children will experience depression before they become adults. Each day in America, fifty young people try to take their own lives. In 2010, there were as many bankruptcies as there were newly minted college graduates. Whatever one's measure of success and happiness, these young people surely don't have it.

However, do not think these are simply the typical challenges of navigating through adolescence that adulthood will change. A 2010 Gallup Poll found that only 20% of adults are passionate about what they do for a living, leaving 80% wishing they were doing something else. It seems that the new status quo is living a life of unrealized dreams. Does it have to be this way? Not according to our research.

We all know people who seem to live a life of great happiness and joy. They've discovered peace and a real sense of meaning in their lives. Their success stands out from the crowd, and while they make up a small percentage of society, there is no reason it has to remain this way. There have always been happy and successful people. We believe that happiness and success are within reach for all of us. What you are about to discover in this book is the result of our revolutionary research and its breakthrough conclusions. We studied some of the happiest and most successful people of all time. We looked at what drove them and what conditions existed that propelled them and allowed them to achieve their Ultimate Lives. Eventually, we saw a definite pattern emerge and were able to identify the individual pieces that produced the pattern of success. It is that pattern that's at the core of this book, what we call the 7 *Mindsets*.

In this book, Jeff and I will share the results of our research, some of which will astound you, and all of which holds the key to helping you achieve your own level of greatness. We hope our discovery will empower and inspire you to live your Ultimate Life. I must warn you, however, that Jeff and I have a hidden agenda. We believe that many of the world's challenges are only going to be solved in the hearts and minds of young people. If we had magic wands, we would empower all youth around the world to live their Ultimate Lives and bring positive change to their communities. Perhaps our magic wand is the content of this book. We believe we can help create a generational shift, one in which young people live to their greatest potential and seek exciting, creative, and meaningful ways to make a positive impact on the world.

Today, I feel like I am much more than just a businessman. When I think back on the nervous, uncertain young man walking into that Newark Boys & Girls Club, I can't help but smile and shake my head. I didn't know exactly what I was going to do for the next two hours, let alone the next two decades. All I knew was that I wanted to help some young people find success. I did that, and am still doing it today. It's been a long journey, but it's been a great one, and it's led me to believe that I can empower millions of people to live their Ultimate Lives.

The 7 *Mindsets* have the power to unlock the door to success and happiness. Jeff and I invite you to explore the unexpected blueprint for an extraordinary life. Empowered by the 7 *Mindsets*, everything is indeed possible.

Scott J. Shickler
Roswell, GA
October 17, 2011

Chapter 1

The Great Paradox

"We cannot solve the problems we face with the same level of thinking that created them."

-Albert Einstein

The Burning Question

If everyone wants to grow up to live a happy and successful life, why do so few achieve it?

This simple question launched a multi-year, multi-million dollar research project. In the first phase of our research, we studied happy and successful people throughout history, hoping to identify important similarities. The second phase of our research uncovered why the majority of people fall short of reaching their desired level of happiness and success. In the third and final phase of our research, we developed a methodology to teach our findings to young people in a meaningful and sustainable way.

The research is groundbreaking, and the results are both surprising and revolutionary. This book contains our findings, as well as a blueprint to live a life of greater potential, meaning and significance. An Ultimate Life is one filled with passion, happiness, and extraordinary success. We will attempt to be as clear and straightforward as possible in demystifying what we learned.

"If you want to know how to get where you want to go, listen to the people coming back from where you want to be."

-Anonymous

History Holds the Answers

The self-help industry generates over ten *billion* dollars a year. There is no shortage of books, CDs, DVDs, and seminars on how to live a better life. Research shows that the majority of typical self-help customers were previous purchasers of self-help material. This is one reason why self-help has been referred to as "shelf-help"—customers don't seem to find solutions that work for them, so they hop from one product to the next, filling their bookshelves along the way.

Many self-help gurus believe that most people are simply hungry and eager to learn more strategies and wouldn't buy self-help products if they didn't work. But in spite of all the self-help strategies being pitched, more and more people seem to be miserable and falling short of their desired goals.

It doesn't help that there is conflicting advice on the subject of personal achievement. It's like finding a needle in a haystack. Where do you begin? What books should you read? The comedian George Carlin once said in a stand-up routine, "I went to a bookstore and asked the saleswoman, 'Where's the self-help section?' She said if she told me, it would defeat the purpose."

Finding the right advice is only part of the challenge. Making the necessary change is what derails most people. So we decided to begin our research studying those who've managed to find the right advice and implement changes in their lives. We have nicknamed this group the *ultra-successful* because they do stand out from the crowd. It was important to research people throughout time, from the famous to the relatively unknown, from all walks of life and regions of the world. You will recognize the names of many people in our research, but we also studied hundreds of seemingly ordinary people who found a way to live lives filled with greater joy and personal achievement than most.

Happiness and success are subjective concepts, but we measured our results according to the norms of the day. We all know people who have money but are miserable. We also know people who seem to have few material luxuries, yet they radiate joy and zest for life. All of these factors were considered as we looked to see if we could find significant similarities. This is not a book that outlines get-rich-quick strategies, or focuses solely on the wealthy and famous. While many of the people we studied believed they had more money in their life then they ever imagined, others showed no real interest in the accumulation of wealth. We were in search of people who found ways to live lives filled with passion, meaning, and a stronger sense of purpose and achievement. What follows is an overview of our research process.

We Studied the Studies

Throughout history, great minds and organizations have analyzed and studied happiness, achievement, and success. We started our research by examining the large body of existing research. We studied the writings of the ancient Chinese masters including Lao Tzu and Confucius. We studied the works and lives of the Greek Philosophers including Aristotle, Plato, and Socrates. We analyzed the works of the Roman Stoic philosophers, including Epictetus and Marcus Aurelius. We reviewed the lives and works of the Middle Eastern philosophers such as Rumi, and the European thinkers including Voltaire, Descartes, and da Vinci. We studied the influential works of the 20th Century Industrial Revolution including those of Napoleon Hill, Dale Carnegie, and W. Clement Stone. Lastly, we analyzed the $50 million research project on global happiness and other research conducted by Dr. Martin Seligman, Director of the Positive Psychology Center at the University of Pennsylvania.

We Read the Landmark Books

With over two million books currently available through Amazon.com, we needed to be selective in our source material. We elected to focus on best-selling titles that have appeared to stand the test of time and critical review. A complete list can be found in the resource section at the back of this book. A sample of the books used in our research includes:

Think and Grow Rich by Napoleon Hill

The 7 Habits of Highly Effective People by Stephen Covey

Man's Search for Meaning by Viktor Frankl

Authentic Happiness by Martin Seligman

The Success Principles by Jack Canfield

The 7 Spiritual Laws of Success by Deepak Chopra

Now Discover Your Strengths by Marcus Buckingham

Good to Great by Jim Collins

Happy for No Reason by Marci Shimoff

The Passion Test by Janet & Chris Attwood

The Alchemist by Paulo Coelho

The Purpose Driven Life by Rick Warren

The Secret by Rhonda Byrne

The Power of Positive Thinking by Dr. Norman Vincent Peale

The Art of Happiness by the Dalai Lama

The Four Agreements by Don Miguel Ruiz

The Power of Now by Eckhart Tolle

Unlimited Power by Anthony Robbins

Maximum Achievement by Brian Tracy

Excuses Begone by Dr. Wayne Dyer

We Analyzed the Ultra Successful

Since the time of the Renaissance, there have been thousands of documented extraordinary lives. We felt it critical that these lives be analyzed to find significant similarities. We researched great artistic minds like da Vinci, Michelangelo, and Shakespeare. We reviewed the philosophies of the some of history's foremost scientific thinkers, including Isaac Newton, Charles Darwin, and Albert Einstein. We examined the iconic American success stories of John Rockefeller, Henry Ford, Thomas Edison, Andrew Carnegie, Cornelius Vanderbilt, J.P. Morgan, and others. We studied the lives of brave social change agents like Gandhi, Mother Theresa, and Martin Luther King, Jr. We analyzed accounts of epic political leaders including Nelson Mandela, Winston Churchill, and Abraham Lincoln. We read the autobiographies and biographies of daring entrepreneurs such as Sir Richard Branson, Bill Gates, and Anita Roddick. We considered celebrated athletes including Michael Jordan, Wilma Rudolph, and Pelé, and the lives of extraordinary artists and entertainers including Oprah Winfrey, Will Smith, Shakira, and others.

We Conducted Live Interviews

Getting to the heart of the matter included interviewing over 400 successful individuals and authors who focus on happiness, achievement, and success. Some of the people interviewed included billionaire Richard Branson; Wally "Famous" Amos; Brian Tracy; Les Brown; Jack Canfield & Mark Victor Hanson, co-authors of the best-selling *Chicken Soup for the Soul* series; Ben & Jerry; Fred DeLuca, founder of Subway; Earl Graves, founder of *Black Enterprise* magazine; Steve Forbes, Editor of *Forbes* magazine; Snowden McFall, author of *Fired Up!;* Dr. Wayne Dyer; Robert Kiyosaki, author of *Rich Dad Poor Dad*; Dr. Dennis Waitley, author of *The Psychology of Winning*; Steve Jobs; Dr. Ken Blanchard, global leadership expert; Cheryl Richardson, co-author of *You Can Create an Exceptional Life;* and Anita Roddick, founder of The Body Shop.

We Researched With Our Students

Our education company has served millions of educators and youth around the world. Additionally, our research team has over 100 combined years working directly with 200,000 teenagers. We have developed knowledge through firsthand experience on the thought patterns, perspectives, and expectations of teens. We understand how youth view happiness and success. We are intimately familiar with the common advice delivered by parents and educators on how to be successful. We understand what motivates students and, of equal importance, the things that demotivate them. It is this youth empowerment expertise that ultimately allowed us to translate our findings into a language and structure both relevant and engaging for teens and adults. Through the years, we have learned to translate sophisticated content into a usable and sustainable form.

The Revolutionary Results

After thousands of hours of research, 400+ interviews, a comprehensive analysis of comparative data from other research projects, and the deconstruction of over 100 books, our results were astounding.

We'll begin by telling you what the happiest and most successful people don't have in common. It's not their gender, ethnicity or where they live in the world. It has nothing to do with whether they came from a loving home or a broken one. It doesn't matter if their family comes from money, is middle class, or impoverished. It's not even connected to how far they advanced in school or the skill sets they acquired along the way. While all of these things seem important, they proved to be only surface attributes. We found resounding evidence that patterns of happiness and success come from both genders and all ethnicities; from the well-educated and the unschooled; from those with means to those without; and from those with loving parents to those who were adopted, abandoned, and even abused.

Equally important is that people who do not view themselves as happy and successful also come from both genders, all ethnicities, loving and dysfunctional homes, households with Ivy League parents and with parents who were high school dropouts, from professional and blue collar homes, and across the wide economic spectrum of the haves and have-nots. The game-changing patterns of happiness and success are not based on your personal history, nor on the common belief that "it's not what you know, but who you know."

Our findings alone can save you a lifetime of heartache. We hope your brain is spinning as our research results challenge much of what's thought of as "conventional wisdom."

What Do the Ultra-Successful Have in Common?

Simply put… it's the way they think. The happiest and most successful people we researched have certain mindsets in common. Specifically, we have identified seven common mindsets. While it was not essential that every research subject possessed all seven mindsets at all times, we did find that the ultra-successful, the happiest and the most accomplished people in the study actively embraced the majority of the mindsets at different points in their lives. We have labeled these commonalities *The 7 Mindsets to Live Your Ultimate Life,* and there is a chapter in this book devoted to each of them.

The Great Paradox

As expected, our research revealed many of the usual predictors of success and happiness in life. What we did not expect was that upon finding a series of mindsets common to those we call the ultra-successful, we also learned that, not only are the vast majority of people not living those mindsets, most are thinking and acting in direct contradiction to them. Evidence suggests that a majority of society is applying what we have labeled *the counter mindsets.* To compound the matter, most teachers and parents teach the counter mindsets, because that's what they have been taught will lead to the good life. Unfortunately, for most people the counter mindsets have become the status quo and eventually drive individuals to lives of moderate success and fleeting happiness, at best.

In the next chapter, we will address the counter mindsets and set the stage for a transformational mind shift–one with the potential to empower you to live your Ultimate Life.

Chapter 2

Change Your Mindset, Change Your Life

"Our environment, the world in which we live and work, is a mirror of our attitudes and expectations."

-Earl Nightingale

It is currently estimated that over one billion children are deprived of food, and over 200 million of them are chronically malnourished. Twice as many people died in the 20th century from war-related violence than did in the 19th century. Most experts now predict that number will double again in the 21st century. The global economy is in turmoil, and many believe we are systematically destroying our planet. In the United States, dropout rates are increasing, depression is growing, and violence and drug abuse continue to be prevalent. At a time when we have more than we have ever had, we seem even more at odds than ever with lives of true happiness and meaning. Worse, we seem to have catastrophic issues with very few answers. If the 7 Mindsets have been around throughout recorded history, why do so many people not fully understand them? And perhaps even more perplexing, why have the majority of people adopted the exact opposite mindsets? This chapter will explain some possible theories and provide a foundation for a positive mind shift.

Let's Go to the Flea Circus

Although a thing of the past, the flea circus started in England around 1830 and grew in popularity in circuses and carnivals around the world for a hundred years, ultimately disappearing from the entertainment landscape by the end of the 1960s. During the height of its popularity, people not only would willingly pay money to watch fleas perform circus acts, but there were people who became professional flea trainers... and it's the flea trainers who help shed some light on the societal issues of our time.

The process of training fleas was quite simple. Dozens of fleas were gathered and placed in a glass jar with a lid. Fleas are known for their ability to jump, but as they naturally jumped inside the jar, they would bang their heads on the lid. After just two days of training, they learned to adjust the height of their jumps so they would avoid banging into the lid. The trainer could then remove the lid of the jar, and the fleas would maintain their same jumping height. They wouldn't even try to escape even though they could still easily clear the confines of the jar.

What's even more interesting is that when the fleas reproduced, they taught their offspring to only jump as high as the imaginary lid. One can only suppose that the parent fleas had the best interest of their babies at heart. After all, who wants their young to experience pain? Little did they know that they were limiting the future potential of generation after generation of fleas.

Virus of the Mind

Every day, a virus wakes up with a simple list of things to do: infiltrate a host, spread throughout the host, infect another host, and repeat... all day, every day. There are biological viruses that are transmitted through human contact. There are computer viruses that carry programs to wipe out data and cause major damage. Perhaps one of the most destructive viruses is called a meme. In his book, *The Virus of the Mind*, Richard Brodie discusses the science of Memetics. Memetics is the study of memes, or mental viruses. Memes are the equivalent of contagious diseases that infect our thinking. Just like any virus, it is their intention to enter, infect, and spread. A meme is simply a thought passed from one person to another. Most of us catch memes from our parents, teachers, and friends. The memes that have survived have been successful at spreading from person to person and from generation to generation. The vast majority of us continue to spread them today, believing at a subconscious level that the memes are valid and indeed help us. This is essentially what has happened throughout history. We have been programmed to our current way of thinking, and most of us find it difficult, if not impossible, to change. Mcmes become mental habits. Some memes are good, and some are destructive viruses that infect the mind and place major limitations on individual potential and society as a whole.

Let's see if you're infected. Can you finish this sentence? *Money doesn't grow on...*

How about this one? *Curiosity killed the...*

Don't worry, if you're infected, we will provide you with the antidote for this troublesome type of meme.

The Counter Mindsets

Imagine a series of memes that you believe in your heart and mind to be true. These gems have been passed down from people who love you and care about you. They have been packaged as little pearls of wisdom and delivered at just the right time with the intention of helping you learn an important lesson. They seem relevant and rational. You even pass them along to your friends and vice versa when the situation calls for a little wisdom. Some of these memes are so powerful that many people share them as if they possess the sacred keys to happiness and success. Unfortunately, the memes we're describing have the opposite result. Our research demonstrates that these memes, what we call the counter mindsets, lead to lives of frustration, under-performance, and a general sense of mediocrity.

The counter mindsets are best seen in the core lessons experienced in childhood, and it is very likely we will pass them on to our own children, unless there is a conscious intervention. For example, we are all familiar with the saying "Money doesn't grow on trees." When parents use this adage, they are trying to teach their child an important lesson about money. Perhaps trying to convey an important connection between hard work, earning, and saving for what you want in life. It is rational thinking and usually given with the best of intentions. Unfortunately, it's like speaking Italian to someone who only understands English. There is a language barrier, and the parent's intention is usually lost in translation.

When kids hear this saying for the first time, it's probably when they want something special... really badly. They don't like hearing "No," which is what the parents are really saying, but in a sugarcoated way. When phrases like that are said over and over, as parents do when trying to pass along a valuable life lesson, the logic of the lesson is lost and replaced with an emotional scar. Unfortunately, we are inadvertently conditioning our youth into an adversarial relationship with money. Money, in their mind (and later found in the DNA of their habits), becomes a very scarce commodity and one that usually evokes negative emotions. It's not too far of a leap to get to the meme, "Money is the root of all evil."

Risky Business

Whether in baseball or business, dating or dominoes, risk is an integral part of success. Taking a chance, especially in the face of potential failure, can be the difference between just surviving and really thriving. Yet here's a meme, a counter mindset we've all heard before, that discourages one of the essential elements of achievement: "Don't make the same mistake twice." When they give this advice, people believe they are teaching children to learn from their mistakes, to continue to grow and expand. When we ask teens what this saying means to them, most say it makes them feel like mistakes are bad. Imagine that Thomas Edison, who failed hundreds of times before finally perfecting the electric light bulb, had embraced that meme. Perhaps you've heard or used the famous meme, "Curiosity killed the cat." To teens, this means, "Mind your own business." Do we really want to raise kids to not be curious? Where would Albert Einstein and Leonardo da Vinci have been if they had turned off their curiosity switches?

It is not our intention to judge parents and teachers. We believe they are doing the very best they can with the greatest intentions for their children and students. Consider for a moment the number of times you may have told a child how proud you are of them. It is certainly something we have done hundreds of times. Now consider how the saying, "I am proud of you" may actually teach children to look externally for validation, something we know to be very detrimental. What if simply saying, "You should be proud of yourself" accomplishes everything you want (making the child feel good), but also teaches them to look inside for validation. It really is the subtle language we use every day that is conditioning our children in the very mental habits that are driving lives of struggle and frustration. What if we could change everything, not by making things harder or requiring more information, but rather by adjusting what we are currently doing and saying? And what if that was the difference between the average life and the Ultimate Life?

"Our life is what our thoughts make it."

-*Marcus Aurileus*

The Scarcity Theory

Henry David Thoreau once said that "The mass of men live lives of quiet desperation." It is a tragic but very true statement. Statistics show that 80% of us do not find fulfillment in our jobs. Current research indicates that depression and suicide are growing at an alarming rate. Experts tell us that more than 45% of marriages end in divorce. The same experts tell us that general discontent continues to grow in society today. In a world of ever-expanding opportunity, a growing percentage of us are finding it very difficult to simply find joy and fulfillment.

The root of all this suffering is a perception of scarcity. A belief that the world's resources are limited has convinced us that our lives have limitations, too. In truth, humans have lived in a scarce world since the beginning of time. We may have been isolated and alone at times, but despite external scarcities, we thrived. We formed tribes that grew into countries; we developed belief systems that evolved into religions; we took general ideas and expanded them until they became philosophies; and we took simple systems of bartering and trading and helped them grow into global business communities.

Humans have, throughout our history, gathered in tribes, countries, ethnic communities, and religious groups, rather than as a single humanity, thus creating group identities. However, for some, these identities have become more acute and potentially divisive. Some become disconnected from other individuals and organizations that threaten the identity. In that posture, life becomes a zero sum game. Fear takes over as we fight for our share. We stay in jobs we dislike because we are afraid we won't find another one, or that one day we will wake up and find out we don't have enough money. We build relationships based on a need for security rather than meaning and fulfillment. We fight with others over perceived scarcity of resources. We struggle to find happiness, we limit our lives, and we rarely achieve our full potential. Perhaps scarcity is just one big meme that we need to release.

We Are Prisoners of Our Five Senses

We live in a world dictated by what we can see, hear, taste, touch, and feel. You're probably familiar with the meme, "Seeing is believing." Is that really true? Our eyes can't see infrared light, yet it does exist. Our human ears can't hear ultrasound, even though a dog can. Current scientific theory maintains that everything in the world we can experience through one or more of our five senses only amounts to 4% of what actually exists. So everything we can see, feel, etc., like mountains, oceans, cars, clothing and people, only adds up to 4% of what actually exists. This means that 96% of the world we live in can't be experienced through one of our five senses! This 96% is often referred to as dark matter. Our five senses limit our view of reality and continue to reinforce our misconception of a world of scarcity. Throughout history, this has been the case. Until the 15th century, most people believed the world was flat. This was simply a combination of the way their eyes perceived the visible world and an old belief system that stated the earth was flat. Once the great explorers demonstrated this to be wrong, a whole new world of exploration and trade was created. Similarly, one day Pluto was a planet, and the next day it wasn't.

Life's Window

Along with what we can perceive with our senses, we are also products of our experiences. Our experiences create our reality, as well as our preconceived notions of how the world works when we interact with it. Imagine that, at the instant we're born, we emerge to see a window. The window is clean and wide open. The world is perfect and full of endless possibilities. Then, around age three, you tell your parents you want to learn to fly. They tell you that only birds and bugs can fly, and that humans were made to walk and run. Your dream of flight is squelched, and the shade on the window is lowered just a bit, limiting your view of life.

Later in life, you raise your hand to answer a question in class. You get it wrong, and the teacher is critical, believing you did not do your homework. You think to yourself, I won't risk that again. So you learn not to take risks, and the window shade lowers a little more. Later in school, you want to try out for a team and your friends tell you that there is no way you'll make the cut. Fearing the ridicule, you don't try out. You want to ask someone on a date, but you tell yourself he or she is out of your league. The window shade lowers and lowers. By the time you are 18, ready to go to college and take on the world, you are looking through a two-inch slit of glass, and your view on life's possibilities has shrunk significantly. The world of opportunity you experienced at birth no longer exists through this distorted perspective. It has been reduced to only a fraction of what it might have been had we still believed in our own unique potential. Nothing is different about the world into which you were born... but your perception has changed.

On a Short Rope

In his groundbreaking book *The Four Agreements,* Don Miguel Ruiz discusses how humans are born into a world of unlimited potential. We then go through an experience similar to that of a circus elephant, in which we're trained into a new reality. When an elephant is born, circus trainers tie one end of a rope around the elephant's leg, and the other end to a stake in the ground. The baby elephant is too weak to pull out the stake, and after just a few weeks it believes it can't break free and gives up trying. Even as an adult elephant with the strength of dozens of men, the elephant believes it can't break free and doesn't attempt to escape. For the rest of its life, the elephant is contained in a world limited by a stake and a short piece of rope. As happens with most humans, the elephant's world has become the limited place they perceive it to be. The world truly is what we believe it is.

The Subconscious Rules

As our experience and senses provide input into our lives, we develop a set of belief systems rooted in our subconscious minds. These belief systems drive our thoughts and feelings. It is our thoughts and feelings that drive the decisions we make and the actions we take. It is our decisions and actions that determine the results in our lives. Fundamentally, our lives are driven by mindsets that dwell at a subconscious level.

The conscious mind can hold about seven pieces of information in short-term memory. The subconscious mind stores everything we have ever learned. *Brain researchers estimate that your unconscious mind outweighs the conscious on a scale of ten million to one.* Science has proven that a subconscious thought travels 800 times faster than light and is 30,000 times more powerful than a conscious thought. Whether we know it or not, the subconscious mind is far more powerful than the conscious mind. From time to time, our conscious mind will actually come in conflict with our subconscious mind. Now you understand why the subconscious wins when this happens.

Think of yourself as a computer with your conscious mind as the keyboard and monitor. That is where the initiating action takes place, and the computer interacts with the world. The subconscious mind is the underlying software. It simply executes as it is programmed. While the conscious mind (the keyboard) is critical, the ultimate power resides in the subconscious mind or software.

Just as a computer virus can infect an operating system and disrupt all functioning, viruses have infected our minds. They are embedded in our subconscious, driving our feelings and beliefs, and in the end, the decisions we make and the actions we take. We are habitually doing things the same way and expecting different results. Some of us may even try to do things differently with little success, ultimately falling back into the same behavior patterns. The foundation of personal achievement and the root of happiness and success lie in our mental habits, or mindsets, that have evolved at a subconscious level. It is through them, and only through them, that true life change and increased personal achievement can occur.

Kick the Habit

Our mindsets form habits, and our habits tend to drive the results in our lives. When something in your life is not going the way you want it to go, then you have to make a change. The good news is that many experts believe you can form a new habit in approximately 21 days. However, what most people don't realize is that it can take 3-6 months to change an existing habit, perhaps even longer depending on how long you've had the habit. This is why so many people fail to make significant changes in their lives, even when they have an idea of what to change. Whether following a diet, a new exercise program, financial advice, or even relationship counseling, you have to stick with it long enough to break the old habits. Most people expect change to happen more quickly and give up too soon, believing that the newfound strategy just isn't working.

Change is hard, no doubt. That is why it is estimated that over 98% of personal change efforts fail. Now, however, we have a proven blueprint to the Ultimate Life. The stakes are big, and the rewards tremendous. A true shot at an extraordinary life is the greatest of all end games. Our research, history, and even science is beginning to prove there is a very predictable and repeatable process anyone can undergo to live their dreams. The *7 Mindsets* are the blueprint.

The Incredible Capacity of the Brain

Your brain is the most complex mechanism in the world, and the most influential organ in your body. It has unbelievable capability. In 1997, new camera technology allowed us to view the brain at levels far exceeding anything ever conceived in the past. For the first time, we could view the activity of the brain at a cellular level *while* it was functioning. In one amazing session, it was seen that brain cells have tiny tentacles protruding from them. Each time you perform a function of any kind, these tentacles make connections referred to as DSPs (Dendrite Spinal Protuberances). Smell a flower and one set of connections is made, blink your eye and different connections are made. The term scientists have used for this is *plasticity*, meaning that your brain acts like plastic that can be re-formed into an almost infinite set of connections.

With this new knowledge, scientists have estimated the total number of brain cells and the total number of new connections (DSPs) that our brain can make. The number they came up with is staggering. Imagine the number 1 followed by enough zeros to fill up an 800-page book. That is a really big number. Now imagine that the last zero went off the last page and was followed by enough 0s to stretch out for 62 million miles. If you can comprehend that number, you can begin to grasp the unbelievable capacity of the human brain. These same scientists have devised a new estimation of our utilization of the brain. They no longer believe that we have tapped into 10% of our brain's potential (as was once thought), nor even 1%; more like 1/1,000,000 of a percent. Simply put, your brain certainly has the capacity to adapt to new mindsets.

Change Your Mindset, Change Your Life

Throughout history, we have gotten bigger, stronger, and faster. Records are broken continually to demonstrate the expansion of human potential. Creativity invigorates business, science, and technology, resulting in an ever-expanding realm of possibilities. Some among us accomplish amazing feats and live extraordinary lives. How is it that some people are able to tap into much greater capacities than the rest of us? How are exceptional athletes and musicians able to achieve such high levels of performance? How was Albert Einstein able to develop theories so advanced that most scientists believe we still would not have uncovered them today, 100 years later? How is Bill Gates able to amass over $40 billion in wealth while 90% of the world struggles to provide their basic necessities? The answers reside in the mental habits we have and the behaviors they drive in our life.

The good news is, our research indicates that you can change a mindset and sustain it. By adopting the *7 Mindsets,* you can positively change the outcomes in your life. We will help you do that throughout this book. The next seven chapters will each be devoted to one of the *7 Mindsets.* You will learn to recognize the counter mindsets, and applying the *7 Mindsets* will lead you toward your Ultimate Life. We will guide you every step of the way, and you will be empowered to choose your path.

The Road Less Traveled

Two roads diverged in a wood, and I—
I took the one less traveled by,
And that has made all the difference.

-Robert Frost

The 7 Mindsets to
Live Your Ultimate Life

Everything Is Possible
Passion First
We Are Connected
100% Accountable
Attitude of Gratitude
Live to Give
The Time Is Now

We chose the names for the *7 Mindsets* carefully so young people (and adults, too) could remember them easily. Don't be fooled into thinking that you fully understand the deep meaning behind each mindset simply by reading its given name. However, once you fully comprehend the explanations we provide in the coming chapters, you will more easily and accurately remember them due to the simplicity of the their names.

Each mindset chapter will include a section called **The Counter Mindsets**. We will describe some of the most common memes that people have inadvertently adopted and are in direct contradiction to the *7 Mindsets*. This will help you identify and ultimately eliminate them from your subconscious.

Mindsets in Action is a special section in each chapter with specific steps you can take to better learn the *7 Mindsets* and begin activating them in your life.

Lastly, each mindset chapter will conclude with a quick summary called **Mindset in a Minute** to provide you with an unexpected blueprint for an extraordinary life.

Chapter 3

Everything Is Possible

"Risk more than others think is safe. Care more than others think is wise. Dream more than others think is practical. Expect more than others think is possible."

-Claude T. Bissell

The Cornerstone of Modern Motivation

Napoleon Hill, a writer born into poverty, worked his way up from a young reporter for a small newspaper to a respected journalist. Hill considered the turning point in his life to have been in 1908, when he was assigned to interview the industrialist Andrew Carnegie as part of a series of articles about famous and successful men. Carnegie was one of the richest and most powerful individuals in the world at the time, and Hill discovered that Carnegie believed the process of success could be outlined in a simple formula that anyone could understand and achieve. Impressed with Hill, Carnegie asked if he was up to the task of putting together this information by interviewing or analyzing over 500 successful men and women, many of them millionaires, in order to discover and publish this formula for success.

As part of his research, Hill interviewed many of the most famous people of the time including Thomas Edison, Alexander Graham Bell, George Eastman, Henry Ford, John D. Rockefeller, Sr., Charles M. Schwab, F.W. Woolworth, William Wrigley, Jr., John Wanamaker, William Jennings Bryan, Theodore Roosevelt, and William H. Taft.

Hill's long-term interview-study culminated in one of the greatest books on personal achievement ever written, *Think and Grow Rich.* We believe it to be the preeminent work on dream fulfillment ever conducted. Ultimately, the book came to a rather simple solution, that success is a function of expectations. Hill concluded that the primary predictors of success are 1) having a clear vision for your life, 2) sustaining a burning desire, and 3) expecting to be successful.

"Whatever the mind can conceive and believe it can achieve."

-Napoleon Hill

We have become forecasters of a different source with our years of experience working with schools and organizations. When we visit a school or an organization, we use our powers of observation and what we know to make a determination of the school or organization's environment. One of the things we look for, or to be more precise, what we attempt to feel in our gut, is how much empowerment is in the air.

In schools and organizations that truly empower their students, the youth have great expectations. There is great clarity in what they want to do with their lives. There are great expectations placed on them by teachers, and the students have great expectations for themselves. After working with over 200,000 teenagers around the world, our research is 100% consistent with that of Napoleon Hill. Our lives are indeed a product of what we expect them to be.

The Final Frontier

Care to go for a ride into outer space? Now you can take a roundtrip for around $200,000. As part of our research, we interviewed Sir Richard Branson. At the end of the interview, he was asked what he would do differently if he could start over again. Without hesitation he responded, "I would dream bigger." If you are not aware of it, Branson is worth over $2 billion. He's started more than 100 companies. Today he lives on his own private island. His two latest ventures are Virgin Galactic, the first company to commercialize space tourism, and Virgin Oceanic, which is taking tourists to the deepest points in the Pacific Ocean. Pretty amazing stuff for someone who thinks his dreams aren't big enough.

Branson was not belittling his accomplishments. As a matter of fact, interviews with hundreds of other successful men and women demonstrate that his feelings are felt by most of the great achievers. When we interviewed Jack Canfield (co-author of *Chicken Soup for the Soul*), he described a survey that asked the most accomplished men and women in the U.S. that same question we asked Branson "What would you do different if you could start over?" Their responses were the same: they would dream bigger, but they would also start sooner.

People like Branson realize that everything which exists in the world today was just an idea in the mind of an individual who was curious enough to wonder. Fire, the wheel, electricity, the automobile, the airplane, and the cell phone were all once only in the world of imagination. But then someone had an idea and believed it was possible to take that idea out of the world of imagination and give birth to it in the real world, making the seemingly impossible possible.

Today, Branson understands that *Everything Is Possible*; that a clear vision and an absolute faith in its possibility will most certainly create a new reality. Once we understand this, as Branson clearly does, we also learn that the only limitations in our lives are our own dreams, expectations, and the time we have to make them happen. So why not dream bigger and start now?

The Counter Mindsets

Have you ever watched the movie *Rudy*? If you have, you know the storyline. If you've never seen it, *Rudy* is the story of a young man of average athletic skills and is on the short side, who has a dream of playing for Notre Dame, one of the legendary college football teams in America. Seeking encouragement from one of the priests in the movie, Rudy gets the advice, "The key to happiness is learning to be happy with what you have."

This is the type of advice usually doled out by parents, teachers, and mentors millions of times each day around the world. It is based on rational thinking, and it has been passed down from generation to generation with one overall intention: to prevent our children from being disappointed. The problem is that such information is garbage.

What would Helen Keller's life have been like had she believed she only needed to learn to be happy with what she had, given her physical limitations? And more importantly, what would Helen's teacher, Anne Sullivan, have believed if she herself had bought into the notion of settling for what was? Together, Helen and Anne proved the world wrong. Anne Sullivan believed that it was possible to teach Helen, and taught Helen to believe it was possible to learn. Helen lived a full and productive life, becoming one of the most inspirational women to ever live.

How about Wilma Rudolph, who had infantile paralysis when she was young? No one ever expected her to walk, let alone become a super-athlete. Wilma Rudolph became the fastest woman in the world, and went on to win three Olympic Gold Medals.

Helen Keller and Wilma Rudolph's lives tell us that the key to happiness is not to settle and be happy with what we've been given, but rather to pursue happiness and believe in what we want.

It is easy to say that Helen Keller and Wilma Rudolph are the exception and not the rule, that they were extraordinary people... and we're just ordinary. While it's true that Keller and Rudolph emerged as extraordinary women, we should never forget that they began life as less than ordinary, but succeeded because they did not accept low expectations for their lives. Why is it that some achieve extraordinary lives while most of us struggle? It is because we have bought into a limited perception of reality. We are so trapped with what we can see, hear, taste, touch, and smell, that we cannot see or believe the world of possibilities that await us.

During World War II, Winston Churchill gave one of his most famous speeches:

We shall go on to the end, we shall fight in France, we shall fight on the seas and oceans, we shall fight with growing confidence and growing strength in the air, we shall defend our Island, whatever the cost may be, we shall fight on the beaches, we shall fight on the landing grounds, we shall fight in the fields and in the streets, we shall fight in the hills; we shall never surrender, and even if, which I do not for a moment believe, this Island or a large part of it were subjugated and starving, then our Empire beyond the seas, armed and guarded by the British Fleet, would carry on the struggle, until, in God's good time, the New World, with all its power and might, steps forth to the rescue, and the liberation of the old.

In a war that seemed lost, it is these words that changed the expectations of a country and ultimately the world. They shifted the collective consciousness and painted a new vision of the future. He gave his people great hope, but more importantly, he changed expectations... and the rest is history.

Mindset in Action: A Step By Step Approach

Step 1: Look inside before you look outside

Everything is Possible is not a naïvely optimistic mindset. It does not mean that a 90-year-old man can be the MVP of his country's World Cup Soccer team. We are not suggesting that you can be the next great scientist (although you may be) or that you will break the world record in the 100-yard dash (although you could). When we ask students to share their dreams, most start out with extrinsically driven dreams like becoming a superstar athlete or rock star. We respond that these dreams may actually happen, but perhaps there is something even better, an expression of their life that is authentic to who *they* are. For every Lionel Messi, one of the world's best soccer players, there are thousands of schoolteachers who live extraordinary lives of joy and meaning and have an enormous impact. The expressions of their lives are equally as powerful as Oprah Winfrey's or Michael Jordan's. They are achieving what we call their *authentic dreams*, a concept we will dive into much deeper later in the book.

The authentic dream first starts deep inside with who you are and what you want. It is these intrinsic aspects that create the foundation from which you can do what seems impossible. The first step to making Everything Possible in your life is to stop allowing external factors and influences to define your dreams. Understand what you stand for and what matters to you. When Walt Disney was a young boy, he lived in an idyllic town called Marceline, Missouri. Disney often called it the greatest time of his life. He loved small town culture and often characterized himself as a small town boy. It was a value he would carry with him his entire life, and a value that ultimately defined much of his work. His found a love for animals in Marceline, which ultimately drove his imagination and his portrayal of animals in his cartoons and feature films. If one visits the Magic

Kingdom in Walt Disney World, you can see that Main Street USA and Tom Sawyer Island are modeled after Marceline, Missouri.

Muhammad Ali once defined his primary value as courage; for Mother Theresa it was compassion; for Albert Einstein, was curiosity. In addition to being a small town boy, Walt Disney defined himself as a dreamer. You can see how centering with one's value creates great strength and focus in life, and how it is the bedrock of great accomplishment.

Step 2: Challenge current thinking

In his book, *How to Think Like Leonardo da Vinci*, Michael Gelb portrays the characteristics of the man some believe to be the greatest genius of all time. One of the seven characteristics that Gelb describes is *Dimostrazione*, an Italian concept meaning, 'a constant seeker of truth with a complete lack of willingness to accept any truths other than those one has observed and concluded on his or her own.' While most think of art and engineering when hearing the da Vinci name, his greatest works were in the area of human anatomy. This work is considered by modern scientists to have been 240 years ahead of his time. In his day, the human body was considered a mystical mechanism. da Vinci, unwilling to accept the then-current dogma, worked with hundreds of animal and human cadavers to uncover such discoveries as how muscles and tendons work, how blood flows through the body, how the major organs work, and how we breathe air and process food. Only through personal observation and self-discovery did da Vinci draw the critical conclusions and create the beliefs that formed his thinking.

In his ground-breaking book *The Four Agreements*, Miguel Ruiz talks about the domestication of humans. He claims we are like animals, having been conditioned by our experiences, and the collective consciousness of our world. He believes that 999 out of 1,000 people are trapped and that only 1 in a thousand has managed to break free. He even calls these rare people "warriors," who continually fight the "parasite" of current mass thinking. In Ruiz's opinion, our only path to true freedom and happiness in life is to break through the barriers of dogma, to challenge all assumptions, and draw our own conclusions through our own experiences.

Albert Einstein was a pacifist who left Germany because he disagreed with the ideology of Nazi Germany. He also unraveled the mysteries of science with theories that challenged the very fiber of our universe. Martin Luther King, Jr. refused to accept the oppression of others, and Gandhi refused to bow to English Imperialism. Monet and fellow Impressionists challenged art and the traditional realist painting approach. The Beatles, Elvis Presley, Ray Charles and others changed everything about music. The great entrepreneurs and business people of our day have succeeded by creating unique products, processes, or business models. Greatness comes from being different, from looking beyond the current views, and expanding into new realms of possibility. This characteristic is essential. One must challenge current assumptions and expand his or her thinking into new realms of possibility.

Step 3: Engage your imagination

Marcus Aurelius is considered one of the five most powerful Roman emperors and possibly the most learned of the Stoic philosophers. Many of his writings were completed on the battlefield as he continually sought greater meaning from life. In one of his classic musings, he stated, "Our lives are dyed with the color of our imagination." What he meant is that our lives, what we achieve, are a product of our ability to envision them.

When most of the world thought computers would never be more than massive mainframes that filled entire floors of building, people like Bill Gates and Steve Jobs imagined a computer in every house. When most thought automobiles would only be a luxury of the rich, Henry Ford imagined the assembly line and produced cars for the common man. It is only through our imagination that we can break out of our current reality. It is impossible to see anything different than what we can see if we do not close our eyes and dream a better dream. We must all cultivate a powerful and highly attuned imagination.

In his book, *A Whole New Mind*, Daniel Pink discusses the critical factors of success for the future. In a world of exponential change, we cannot even fathom the world and challenges that will face our children. Pink argues that any job that is routine will be marginalized and automated. He believes the imaginative, creative mind will no longer be a luxury, but a necessity for any form of success in the future. Albert Einstein once said, "We cannot solve the problems we face at the same level of thinking that created them." It is only through our imagination that we can solve the complex problems we face and deal with the volatile and dynamic nature of the new world.

Step 4: Put your imagination into action

Creativity can be defined as putting our imaginations into action. Seeing a different reality is one thing, but taking action on it is another. Martin Luther King, Jr. had a dream in which his children would be judged by the content of their character, not the color of their skin. It was a big dream with many personal dangers and pitfalls, but he acted on it. He once said, "You do not have to see the entire staircase, you must simply take the first step." King took those steps, because without purposeful and creative action, nothing can change.

Thomas Edison, the American inventor of the light bulb, failed many times when trying to perfect sustainable lighting. When asked how he could keep going, he said, "I have not failed, I've just found 10,000 ways that won't work." Edison, like all celebrated achievers, understood that fantastic accomplishments and notable lives are the culmination of thousands and thousands of tiny steps. Many of the steps, and very likely most of them, are riddled with mistakes, but it is the creative process that is critical.

Look around you. Everything in your life is the product of a creative process. Someone had a dream inspired by their imagination and made it a reality through creative action. We must act on our imagination and ultimately on our dreams. We must have the courage to fail, and understand that every step we take has meaning and is part of the process of fulfilling our dreams.

Step 5: Dream big! Expect great success, happiness, and meaning

We have studied the famous successes, but we have also analyzed the happiest people we know, those people everyone wants to be around and for whom everything always seems to work out. And our consistent conclusion is that they are happy because they expect to be happy. They find meaning because they constantly seek it in every person they meet, every experience they have, and every meal they eat. Happiness and meaning are things they have envisioned their entire lives. And expecting happiness is simply another type of dream, a really big dream, if you think about it.

Michelangelo once said, "The greater danger for most of us lies not in setting our aim too high and falling short, but in setting our aim too low, and achieving our mark." Like others, he saw a world filled with people who expected too little of themselves and their lives. They saw the lives of their parents and those around them, and could never see any further. True happiness and meaning does not come from an absence of failure, but from accomplishment. They come with the expression of one's ability to maximize their potential. As Eleanor Roosevelt once said, "The future belongs to those who believe in the beauty of their dreams."

The vast majority of us have no comprehension of our potential. Recent brain research now demonstrates that we use much less than 1% of our brain's capacity. We are all capable of unbelievably amazing things, but, unfortunately, most of us lock ourselves into a drastically limited view of our world and abilities.

There is a story about actor Jim Carrey, who, while struggling as a new comedian, wrote a check to himself for ten million dollars for acting services rendered. He post-dated the check for ten years later and carried it around in his wallet every day to reaffirm his dream.

Almost to the date, ten years later, he found out he was being paid $10 million to star in the movie *Dumb and Dumber*. Carrey later became the first actor to receive $20 million for his acting services in one movie.

The happiest and most successful people who have ever lived had higher expectations for their lives. Typically, from an early age, they had a very clear and positive image of their future. More importantly, they had a confidence or inner knowledge that they could and would realize their dreams. They may have never stated it explicitly or even thought it, but when asked, they always say that they just knew it would happen.

Step 6: Don't worry about the how

Very few people would take a cross-country road trip without planning ahead. Most likely, they would plan attractions to visit, hotels for lodging, clothes to pack, a budget for meals, and maybe make a playlist for their iPod. The same can be said for embarking on a new business venture. It's prudent to think and plan ahead to avoid mistakes and increase your odds of success. Perhaps this is why one of the toughest challenges people face is letting go of the *how* when it comes to pursuing their dreams.

Many millionaires went bankrupt before they made their first million. Home run kings in baseball usually lead the league in strikeouts as well. Failure provides feedback, and the best way to get feedback is to take action. It's okay to create a plan for the pursuit of your dreams, but it is counter-productive to wait until all aspects line up properly because they never do. They line up along the journey through a maze of trials and tribulations that are impossible to predict. It's only at the achievement of a great accomplishment that one can look back and see the perfectly imperfect path that led you to your goal.

It's okay to have confidence in the unknown. Start getting comfortable with ambiguity. In a world where most people are rooted in reality, the path to their dreams is not always clear. Focus on the *what* and the *why*, but don't worry about the *how*. We get so hung up thinking we must have a clear plan, but a plan cannot possibly understand the creative steps required to make our dreams a reality. We have to believe in our dreams and our ability to overcome all obstacles along the way. We must be able to recognize the amazing opportunities presented to us each day, opportunities that cannot be envisioned or expected.

In their book *The Passion Test*, Janet Bray Atwood and Chris Atwood use a powerful technique when teaching others to visualize their dreams. When defining a goal or dream, they wrote that we need to identify what it is we think we want and then add "or something better" at the end of the statement. With this simple technique, you can ensure your dreams are never limited by your current reality.

Step 7: Be wary of dream snatchers

The last critical step in making *Everything Is Possible* true in your life is to become ever vigilant. We have to recognize that our dreams are precious and need to be protected. And we must be vigilant because our dreams often need protection from the people who claim to know what's best for us, and who don't want us to become disillusioned or disappointed if our dreams die. We must also be on constant guard against the people who not only dislike our optimism, but are actually jealous of our ability to dream, and want nothing more than to shoot our dreams out of the sky.

These dream snatchers often masquerade as friends, but we must be conscious and alert for the negativity a dream snatcher can spread. By recognizing who these dream snatchers are, we can limit their power and not be deterred from our dreams and the critical actions we must take to make them a reality.

He Wishes For the Cloths of Heaven

HAD I the heavens' embroidered cloths,
Enwrought with golden and silver light,
The blue and the dim and the dark cloths
Of night and light and the half-light,
I would spread the cloths under your feet:
But I, being poor, have only my dreams;
I have spread my dreams under your feet;
Tread softly because you tread on my dreams.

-W.B. Yeats

Mindset in A Minute

Everything Is Possible

Dream Big, Embrace Creativity, and Expect Great Results

Step 1. Look inside before looking outside: Build your life and your dreams from a position of strength. Base them on your values and the things that are important to you. It is from this intrinsically motivated perspective that you can act with courage and sustain the burning desire required for greatness.

Step 2. Challenge current thinking: As soon as you accept another's reality, you have limited your own. Become a seeker of knowledge through your own experiences and see the world from your viewpoint. It is this perspective from which you can build a new reality with your life that expands beyond the limitations of your current surroundings.

Step 3. Engage your imagination: Train yourself to visualize and see new realities. Never make assumptions about impossibilities, simply have the courage to imagine and believe. It's through our imagination that we can start the process of improving upon the realities of today.

Step 4. Put your imagination to work through creativity: Build the courage to act on your ideas and dreams. Every action has an equal and opposite reaction. The most powerful actions are purposeful and creative. It is only through trial and discovery that we can traverse the path to our goals and dreams. We must act on our imagination.

Step 5. Expect success, happiness, and meaning: You must build confidence in your ability to live your dreams, achieve greatness, and most importantly, find happiness and meaning in your life. When you expect these things, you will start to recognize the little things each day that indicate your success. The momentum in your life builds, and your life begins to accelerate in a positive direction toward your goals and dreams.

Step 6. Don't worry about the how: Let go of the need to see exactly how you will make something happen in your life. Often the required steps cannot possibly be known because they are not a part of your current experiences and knowledge base. Have courage in the creative process and constantly identify and act on opportunities that align with your goals and dreams.

Step 7. Be wary of dream snatchers: be vigilant with your dreams. Understand that they are precious assets. Recognize when they are threatened and overcome the pressures to let go.

"The future belongs to those who believe in the beauty of their dreams."
-Earl Nightingale

Chapter 4

Passion First

"Many things in life will catch your eye, but only a few will capture your heart –follow those."

-Unknown

The Seed of Life

If money didn't matter, what would you do for free? How would you spend your days? What business would you start? What career would you pursue? What would fill your life with joy? When we speak to teenagers, they easily answer these questions, although usually their first responses are to become superstar athletes, rock stars, celebrities, and mega-mogul zillionaire entrepreneurs. College students have a little more trouble answering, as it seems in direct conflict with what major they may be pursuing and what job interviews they have lined up. Most adults, frankly, are stymied by these questions. It's as if the part of their brain that once dreamed of such wonderful things has turned dormant. It's no wonder that, according to a recent Gallup Survey, approximately 80% of adults say they are not passionate about what they do for a living.

Imagine for a moment that you are born with a special and unique seed inside of you. You might think of it as your *soul seed* or your *passion seed.* Throughout your life, this seed evolves, and growing with it is your unique calling. You can choose to ignore it or perhaps only care for it on the weekend. But it will not go away. You will constantly be reminded of who you are capable of becoming. Many adults experience a mid-life crisis, a time in their life when they pause and ask the questions, "Is this all there is? Is this why I'm here?" The mid-life crisis doesn't discriminate. It hits people with affluence, who wonder why money hasn't bought them the real happiness they seek. It hits people who are struggling, forcing them to wonder if they settled too often in life. These are times to re-examine your life and the choices you made, to start over with greater purpose, to listen to your passion seed... finally!

The Quarter-Life Crisis

According to authors Alexandra Robbins and Abby Wilner, there is now such a thing as a quarter-life crisis affecting young people in their twenties. Here's a remarkable depiction from one of their readers.

I have always referred to this time in my life as my "mid-twenties" crisis. Everyone I know that's my age is in the same thing unless they majored in Business or Computer-related things and got a dream job right out of college. The rest of us are floating around aimlessly trying to find a niche. An undergrad degree is worthless most of the time, and so we end up in dead-end jobs we aren't happy in. We question our dreams, we wonder if we are settling or giving up, or if we should still carry out our dreams, or just let them be "dreams." It is hard to decipher whether or not reality is "giving up" or reality is just plain reality. Then again, you hear about people like Mozart, and Brittney Spears, and Jessie Jackson and other people in this world that achieve their "impossible" dreams... you wonder if it is blind luck on their part, or if they just did something we haven't figured out yet.

There's no need to wonder anymore. Our research clearly indicates that finding your passion and organizing your life around who you are meant to be is the clearest path to living your dreams. In a recent interview that ended Oprah's 25-year talk show, Oprah advised that we follow our passions, for if we do not, we literally cannot truly be happy.

To Be or Not to Be

Shakespeare once wrote, "This above all else, to thine own self be true." Perhaps no more powerful a statement has ever been made, for true happiness is found when we find our authentic self. Lao Tzu is the author of the *Tao Te Ch'ing*. It is believed by many that Lao Tzu was a records keeper who maintained the spiritual teachings of the Eastern masters from China in the 6th Century BCE. The Tao, therefore, was the culmination of one of the most prolific periods of enlightenment in history. In one passage from his powerful work, he states, "At the center of your being you have the answer; you know who you are and you know what you want." Lao Tzu later wrote, "To know others is wisdom, to know yourself is enlightenment." Science has proven that we are unique, that no one has ever existed like us or ever will. We are each a completely unique expression of human life. Our purpose is to find our unique genius, build the courage to pursue it, and share that genius with the world to the maximum extent possible.

"The two greatest days in your life are the day you are born and the day you discover why."

-William Barclay

The Counter Mindsets

In the movie *Jerry McGuire,* there is a scene in which actor Cuba Gooding, Jr. forces his agent, played by Tom Cruise, to yell "Show me the money!" A professional football player, Cuba wants validation of his talent in the form of a large contract with a top-tier team. This mindset is rooted in the very fiber of the free world: an extrinsically-driven motivation that sees wealth creation as life's true measuring stick. On many occasions, all of us make decisions that put money first, resigning our intrinsic characteristics and desires to a secondary role.

Common advice young people receive when choosing a college, selecting a major, and even applying for a job is to think of the future opportunities their choices will provide. Which college will help set them up for a good job? What subjects will prepare them for broader career options? Which job offers more money, better benefits, and room for growth? These are all rational thoughts, but according to our research, they are the wrong questions to ask. Putting money first is almost always the path to a life void of real passion and lowered expectations.

Instead of putting money first, lead with what you would do for free. What subjects give you the greatest joy? What work inspires you? What comes easy to you and is difficult for others? The intersection of your passions and your talents will get you started on the path to an extraordinary life. People who put their passions first tend to work harder than those who don't love what they do. Those with passion learn more, put in the extra time (not because they have to but because they want to), become experts in their fields, are more enjoyable to be around, and are determined to hang in there when times get tough. That's why the ultra-successful all said that when they followed their passion, they ended up making more money than they thought was possible. The joke is on everyone else, though, because most of them admit that they would have done their work for free.

There is a saying: "In life, you can choose either security or freedom, and if you choose security, you will have neither." Too many of us are giving up our dreams in pursuit of the unattainable. We have researched many interviews with folks of tremendous wealth, and the common thread is that money will not make you happy. What makes a person happy is the most fundamental currency: meaning in life. Money can facilitate attaining access and accumulating goods, but money should never be the primary driving force. Happiness comes from doing what you love, with people you love doing things with, and having a great sense of accomplishment and meaning from what you do. People chase success when it's significance they really seek. When you live your *Passion First*, then true happiness is the journey, not the destination.

Passion, in addition to your personal interests, is also driven by what matters to you. If done right, your goals and dreams should drive the results you want to have in your life. In other words, the fruits of your passionate labor must create things and impact people that matter to you in a profound manner. No matter what your chosen vocation, great success and meaning will require the overcoming of massive hurdles and obstacles along the way. If the results do not matter enough to you, somewhere along the way you will stop, and the dream will never be fulfilled.

Mindset in Action: A Step By Step Approach

Step 1: Play to your strengths

Aristotle was the student of Plato, and the teacher of Alexander the Great in ancient Greece. He, along with Plato and Socrates, are the primary drivers of the "Greek Miracle," the first philosophers who transitioned Western society from believing in mythology to rational thinking. Along with his student, Alexander the Great, scholars consider Aristotle to be one of the most brilliant minds who ever lived. Very few, if any, of equivalent intelligence have studied human nature and achievement at the level of Aristotle. Our favorite of his teachings is summed up in his quote, "Where the needs of the world and your talents cross, therein lies your vocation." What Aristotle taught us over 2300 years ago was a pretty straightforward concept of playing to your strengths.

In his book, *Now Discover Your Strengths*, Marcus Buckingham describes a culture of focusing on and minimizing our weaknesses. Supported by extensive research, he tells us that corporations focus their employees on trainings that help them to overcome their shortcomings. Buckingham urges our schools and organizations to become strength-based, leveraging the individual strengths of its people to achieve maximum success and productivity.

Howard Gardner, a developmental psychologist, is critical of our school systems, which currently teach and assess our students in only two primary areas of intelligence (linguistic and logical/mathematical). In his *Theory of Multiple Intelligence*, he argues that there are nine areas in which individuals can and should excel (he adds spatial, kinesthetic, musical, inter- and intra-personal, naturalistic, and existential). Sir Ken Robinson, author of the bestselling book *The Element*, agrees with Gardner that the current state of education is systematically eliminating much of the true talent that exists in our youth. He jokingly debates Gardner, saying there are far more than nine intelligences, more like six billion, or the equivalent of the current number of people on our planet.

The Johnson O'Connor Foundation is a leader in helping youth and adults uncover their natural talents and abilities. While most people look for the obvious strengths such as math, music, art, or athletics, the Johnson O'Connor assessment goes much deeper. They look not only at the most obvious aptitudes, but seek a deeper understanding of one's talents. They seek to answer such questions as 'in what type of situations does one perform best?' and 'with what types of people does one work the best?' It is this type of understanding that truly allows one to attain optimum achievement. What time of day are they the most creative? Are they good under pressure or do they need harmony? Do they accomplish more in groups or alone? We must attain this level of understanding in ourselves before we can truly unleash our potential to its fullest.

Learn to identify your strengths and search for ways to improve them and align them with your day-to-day life.

Step 2: Pursue your passions

In his great book, *The Alchemist,* Paulo Coelho tells the story of a young boy on a journey to discover his "Personal Treasure." The personal treasure was, essentially, the boy's reason for living, the purpose of his life, rooted in that which mattered to him and about which he was passionate. It is a very simple concept, known and passed down for thousands of years. Greatness and genius are the offspring of one's ability to focus. Albert Einstein once said, "It is not that I am more intelligent, it is only that I am passionately curious." It was a consuming desire to understand, not his genius, which guided Einstein to revolutionize our understanding of the universe. His ability to focus on the problem came from a deep-rooted passion to solve it. If you want to achieve greatness, you must align with your passion. It is passion that will motivate you to do all the things required for greatness. You will read more, practice more, learn from others more, and achieve more. Those are the means by which your life will have deeper meaning.

Finding your passion is an extremely introspective process. It requires trial and error, and the constant building of a deeper awareness of oneself. We would argue that it is a never-ending process because your wants, needs, and desires are always evolving. The important thing is that you seek to identify your passion, and then pursue it with courage. If you think you are passionate about making music, take a guitar or piano lesson and find out. If you find that cooking food is something you enjoy, see if you can take it to the next level by working at a restaurant or preparing extravagant meals for guests in your home. Every day of your life should be a constant pursuit of your own "Personal Treasure."

Step 3: Connect your uniqueness to the world around you

The story of Bill Gates is described by Malcolm Gladwell in his book, *Outliers*. Gates and his counterpart, the late Steve Jobs, founder of Apple, were the primary catalysts of the computer and software revolutions. Both were extremely intelligent and both had a true passion for emerging technology. What drove their success was timing. They both happened to be 25 years old in 1980. At that time, technology was ready for a revolution. What was needed was someone young enough to be progressive in his thinking, yet mature enough to understand the practical realities of business. Gates and Jobs both fit that profile, and the rest is history. Each enjoyed overwhelming success connected to his unique genius, but equally critical was how they both applied their intellects.

Throughout history, the most significant triumphs have been a product of timing. Nelson Mandela and Gandhi appeared during a time when countries and their people were ready to separate from England. Martin Luther King was there when Rosa Parks decided not to move to the back of the bus. Abraham Lincoln led our nation through the Civil War, and Anne Frank's presence in an attic transformed our understanding of the Holocaust. Michelangelo gilded the Renaissance, and Mother Theresa served an impoverished India.

We must look inside to uncover our own unique genius, but we must look outside to understand how to impact the world in the most positive manner. This takes courage, because you may be treading on new ground. The world may not initially receive you with open arms. People like what's familiar, and often reject new ideas. Early focus groups hated the search engine name, Google, simply because it was foreign to them. Now it's not only a household name, but also a verb. Henry Ford once commented that if he asked his potential customers what they wanted, they would say a faster horse. Be prepared to be a pioneer as you look to connect your unique genius to the world around you.

Step 4: Build your authentic dream

People often criticize as tyrants the leaders of the American Industrial Revolution. John D. Rockefeller, J. P. Morgan, Andrew Carnegie, and others are often portrayed as greedy individuals who created great wealth at the expense of others. Studies of these individuals shows there are certainly aspects of their lives and character that one could question. What cannot be questioned are their achievements, and the unwavering commitment they had to succeed. All these men had more money than they needed, and most gave all of it away to charities. The ultimate driving force for each of them was the impact their monopolies would have on the world. Cornelius Vanderbilt, for example, believed nothing was more important than an interconnected network of railroads that would facilitate trade and spawn economic growth. The vision and dream of this was at the very fiber of his existence. It was of the utmost importance. The same can be said about J. P. Morgan and banking, Andrew Carnegie and steel, Rockefeller and oil, or Henry Ford and the automobile.

You will hear people say that nothing comes easy. It is true that whatever your endeavor in life, there will be complexities and challenges along the way. For Michael Jordan, his obstacle was the Detroit Pistons. For three years they had beaten his team, the Chicago Bulls, in the playoffs and gone on to the championship. John Daly, the coach of the Pistons, had devised a special defense solely to stop Jordan. In *The Jordan Rules* by Sam Smith, the author details a defense that basically beat Jordan up for four quarters. Jordan responded with greater determination. He rebuilt his physique and became stronger. He developed an outside shot, and his team defeated the Pistons in 1991 and went on to win the NBA title.

You must develop authentic dreams; visions and goals that matter to you, that you believe are of the highest importance. It may be the development of your children, or it could be an NBA championship. The point is, the only way to overcome all the obstacles and challenges you'll encounter is for the dream to matter enough to give you the courage, motivation, and perseverance to break through. Actor Will Smith believes that you need to find a purpose so important that you are willing to die for it. It has to matter that much for you to make it happen. Real passion comes from pursuing authentic dreams that burn like a raging fire deep inside you.

Step 5: Lean in to your passion

In their book, *The Passion Test*, the authors suggest making decisions in favor of what you're passionate about. When deciding between two jobs, choose the one that is more closely aligned with your passion. Trying to decide what class to take? Choose in favor of your passion. Looking to start a business? Before you do, think about what you are most passionate about. Scott's brother, Jadd, is passionate about music. He went on a music-related job interview and thought it was a perfect match. Then he learned that the company didn't have money to hire anyone at that point, and were only doing some preliminary research. Jadd asked Scott for advice. Scott suggested that if Jadd really liked the opportunity, then perhaps he could volunteer some of his time. The rationale was that at least he would be surrounding himself with people and work about which he was passionate. Scott told him to not worry about the money, and to just have fun.

One day while Jadd was volunteering, an opportunity came up for him to shoot a music video with his band, something he had always wanted to do. Not only did he find out about this opportunity because he was volunteering that day, but the video was produced at almost no cost because it was part of a contest. Jadd was in the right place at the right time. Is this a coincidence, or is it the natural by-product of leaning into your passion? It's important to remember that when you do lean in, keep both eyes open and look for signs that allow you to continue choosing in favor of your passion.

Step 6: Embrace your destiny

In his book, *The Seven Spiritual Laws of Success*, Deepak Chopra introduces the concept of Dharma, an ancient Sanskrit term that captures what is meant by the mindset *Passion First*. Inside each of us is a *soul seed*, a boundless capacity, and a wonderful gift to share. Our primary purpose in life is to search within ourselves and uncover this unique genius, then express and share it with the world. It is through our Dharma that we will create the most value with our lives and derive the most joy and meaning in return. We must uncover the soul seed and nurture it. If we can do this, we will reap a lifetime of joy and bliss.

This joy and bliss do not come without some cost. We must sustain the constant courage to act on our destiny. At times, that may mean suffering or being ridiculed. Through your self-discovery process, you may find your unique genius is not what you thought you wanted. It may not fit in or be cool. It may challenge current thinking and be resisted by others. The people you love may not agree with you, and might try to persuade you to go in other directions. To be great, we must be different, and different is not always comfortable.

Every story of success and happiness contains challenge and suffering. Bill Gates dropped out of Harvard to pursue his dream. It is doubtful that many felt that was in his best interest. Abraham Lincoln saw his country suffer around his purpose of preserving a single unified country. People laughed at Wilma Rudolph, who as a crippled young girl, talked of becoming the fastest woman in the world. Pursuing your passion requires you to make difficult decisions, ones that align with your authentic dreams and might push other dreams or relationships to the side. Many times, decisions you make that align with your passion may not seem financially sound. Concern may grow with how you will support yourself and how you can meet the basic necessities of life. The point is, you must trust your genius. You must relish the uncertainty, knowing you can and will succeed. You must embrace your destiny and be fully committed to doing whatever it takes to pursue your passion.

"Do not wish to be anything but what you are, and try to be that perfectly."
-St Francis of De Sales

Mindset in A Minute

Passion First

Pursue your authentic talents and deepest interests

Step 1. Play to your strengths: You will be much more successful doing things at which you excel. This also means putting yourself in situations and environments in which you thrive, and with people that bring out the best in you. Understand your strengths and align what you do with where you can create the most value.

Step 2. Pursue your passions: You can only achieve greatness doing things in which you are interested. Through your passion, you will sustain the focus and do the things that need to be done to overcome obstacles and achieve greatness. Identifying and pursing your talents is a lifelong journey!

Step 3. Connect your uniqueness with the world around you: Your talents and passions can only be utilized if they are put in action creating value. Constantly seek out ways that your abilities and interests can be applied in the world to create value.

Step 4. Build your authentic dream: With an understanding of your unique genius and the needs of the world, redefine your dreams. Make sure the outcomes of those dreams are of the most critical importance to your life. If your dreams matter enough to you, this will be the fuel to overcome the obstacles and challenges you'll face.

Step 5. Lean in to your passions: When you are confronted with a difficult decision, weigh the options and choose in favor of your passion. It's never too soon or too late to start pursuing your passions. Dreams have no expiration date.

Step 6. Embrace your genius: You must find great pride in who you are and what your life is all about. Embrace your destiny and trust your genius to move forward toward the life of your dreams.

"What lies behind us and what lies before us are tiny matters compared to what lies within us."

-Ralph Waldo Emerson

Chapter 5

We Are Connected

"If you can accomplish your dream alone, then you are not dreaming big enough."

-Scott Rigsby

I Was Just Thinking About You!

Have you ever experienced the phenomena of thinking about a friend or family member you haven't seen or spoken with in a long time, then within hours or days, they call you, seemingly out of the blue? We ask this question to hundreds and thousands of people in large presentation rooms and are always amazed at how many people raise their hands. We researched various scientific reasons for this, and some of what we uncovered is mind-boggling, from *quantum entanglement* to *the DNA phantom effect*. However, this book is about mindsets, and sometimes you just need to lean into a mindset long enough for you to experience the personal evidence you require.

In the case of the above-mentioned phenomena, there appears to be something going on that, for now, we'll call *We Are Connected*. At its core, this mindset is about learning to work with, for, and through others to create better lives. In reality, it goes much deeper than that, because it addresses all our relationships, from those characterized by a deep and permanent bond to those that may even seem casual and meaningless.

This chapter will show you how to leverage this unique connection to others.

In his book, *The Butterfly Effect*, Andy Andrews, a New York Times best-selling author and expert on personal achievement, talks about being very curious why some people can just never catch a break. According to them, their lives are in the pits, and it just seems to get worse and worse. Andy jokingly says, "They're right!" He then compares these hapless individuals to other people we all know whose lives always turn up roses. Good things seem to be attracted to them, and their lives just get better and better. Andy then repeats "And they are right!" After years of study, Andy believes the answer to his question is very simple: "The people living great lives are the types of folk that others want to be around. They constantly make positive and meaningful connections, and they use relationships to constantly expand their own happiness and success."

Everyone who comes into our lives has a skill, a unique perspective, or some piece of knowledge that is essential to fulfilling our dreams. Next time you meet someone, test it out. Deliberately engage him or her in a conversation to find out, how can this person help you live your dreams? It could be something as small as the fact that they know someone who can help you fix a leaky faucet, or it could lead to a deeper connection with someone that could ultimately prove life-changing, like connecting you with critical business partners or a companion. We believe you will find the reason your paths crossed, and that the synergy, if leveraged, will take you a step closer to your Ultimate Life.

The Counter Mindsets

You've probably heard the expression, "It's a dog eat dog world," implying that we are in direct competition with one another. Perhaps you can remember a parent, teacher, or friend telling you, "If you want something done right, you have to do it yourself." Over a short period of time, we all seem to have built a world where perceived strength comes from complete independence and autonomy. To become a *self-made man* has been perceived as a great compliment. While the outcome (achieving our goal) might be beneficial, the path to success does not have to be one of solitude. In fact, our research proves that those who have achieved extraordinary success have emphatically stated they could not have done it alone.

We are truly connected, and it is those connections in our lives that help us follow our individual paths. Going it alone might seem to be more courageous, but so much time can be wasted if we isolate ourselves and fail to see how much further we can go if we just reach out.

There's no denying that life can be tough. M. Scott Peck, the author of the mega-selling book, *The Road Less Traveled,* begins by telling his readers that life is difficult. How much more difficult do we make it when we don't tap into the wealth of positive life experiences being offered to us from others if we only take the time to make connections?

Mindset in Action: A Step By Step Approach

Step 1: Create a Sense of Connectedness

The first step to living the *We Are Connected* mindset is the most difficult but the most essential. Too many of us today feel alone. We have isolated ourselves from others and the world around us. Michael Gelb, the Leonardo Da Vinci historian, describes interconnectedness as one of Da Vinci's defining qualities, and one that was instrumental to his success. Leonardo was one of the first "system" thinkers. His passion for anatomy was driven by the curiosity to understand how all the body's organs work together to create and support life. da Vinci was a strong believer in the concept of "Yin and Yang," an Asian philosophy based on the idea that polar opposites or seemingly contrary forces are interconnected and interdependent in the natural world. One commonly held belief is that the Mona Lisa was da Vinci's favorite painting, precisely because it embodied the perfect harmony of humanity and nature.

The first step is to lean into the feeling that there is deeper meaning in all relationships and in all things around the world. The greater sense of connectedness you feel can then inspire you to seek out synergies and meaning in all your relationships. It might help if you lean in to the feeling that everything happens for a reason, and everyone comes into our lives for a reason. Then you will value all of your experiences with a heightened sense of awareness, and look to squeeze much more meaning and joy from your life.

Step 2: Choose Empowering Relationships

In his book, *The Art of Exceptional Living*, Jim Rohn said, "You are the average of the five people you spend the most time with." Statistically speaking, folks who are unhappy hang out with unhappy people. People who struggle financially spend most of their time with others who are struggling. People who get divorced very likely have friends or family members who are divorced. Birds of a feather do flock together. Consider closely those with whom you spend your time. Always consider what influences they have on you, and whether they're building you up or breaking you down. Are your friends and coworkers empowering you or bringing you down? Are you empowering them to live their best lives? Think how inspirational it would be to have a close circle of people regularly supporting and empowering one another to greater levels of achievement and joy.

Step 3: Embrace Competition

In 2009, Tiger Woods was competing with Padrig Harrington in the Bridgestone Invitational golf tournament. At the time, Tiger was number one in the world; and Harrington was considered by many to be the number one contender to the throne. The tournament came down to the final nine holes, and everyone prepared for an amazing competition between golf's two best players. On the 16th hole, Woods trailed by one shot. A notoriously slow player, Harrington was warned by the officials that if he did not speed up play, he would be penalized. Uncharacteristically, Harrington became flustered and made a triple bogey on the hole, essentially handing the tournament to Woods.

After the tournament, Woods was interviewed. The reporter asked Tiger about the back nine and competing with Harrington. Visibly frustrated, Woods criticized the actions that were taken against Harrington in an effort to speed up his slow play on the 16th hole. What frustrated Woods the most was the lost opportunity he had to compete at the very highest level with one of the best golfers in the world.

Regardless of Tiger Wood's lifestyle, no one denies how dominant he was at his craft for over a decade. Many, including most golfers, consider him the greatest golfer and one of the most talented athletes to ever play any sport. Most of us would have been thrilled with an easy victory. Sure, we might have felt a little sorry for Harrington, but deep down, we would be ecstatic that we won the trophy and took home the big check.

Athletes like Tiger Woods and Michael Jordan see competition differently. For them, competition is the catalyst to greatness. It is only through playing with the best at their best that they can ultimately become better; and only by becoming better can they truly feel the great sense of meaning that we all desire. Tiger Woods saw the competition with Padrig Harrington as an opportunity. Not an opportunity to get a trophy or win some money, but to learn something and push himself to do his very best under the most stressful circumstances. It was an opportunity for him to grow and become a better golfer.

Step 4: Relish Diversity

In her book, *Team of Rivals,* Doris Kearns Goodwin tells the story of Abraham Lincoln and a number of political adversaries he defeated in the 1860 presidential election. Lincoln's venomous and one-time political adversaries, Edward Bates, Salmon P. Chase, and William H. Seward didn't fade from view after the election. Instead, Lincoln appointed his opponents to the cabinet level positions of Attorney General, Secretary of the Treasury, and Secretary of State. While most newly elected presidents would have banished their adversaries, Lincoln understood the great genius these men possessed. Further, he recognized that their many political strengths would be vital as he led the country into Civil War.

Instead of separating from his adversaries, Lincoln invited each to join his cabinet. What followed were some of the most intense and heated discussions any president has ever endured. What ultimately resulted were decisions and a collective fortitude that saved the union and kept the United States *united.*

Too often, we identify ourselves with a group or a way of thinking. Once it becomes part of our identity, we resist other groups or ways of thinking because we believe they threaten the very fiber of who we are. da Vinci once said, "I do not care that I am right, what I care about is getting the right answer." That is the essence of what embracing diversity means. We suggest you relish different viewpoints and perspectives and have healthy constructive debates. This may help you come to conclusions and decisions that will be much more effective than the ones you could conceive on your own.

Step 5: Build Your Dream Team

Author Andy Andrews says, "All opportunities and new knowledge come through others." Imagine believing that everyone you come in contact with in your life is critical to helping you live your dreams. Knowing this, you would enter every encounter and every relationship with a heightened sense of energy and preparedness. People would find greater joy in being around you.

Your interactions would become richer and your relationships more meaningful. You would consistently seek and find synergies with others. You would constantly find new opportunities and gain knowledge that you previously would have missed. Your life would become richer in every way.

In Andrews' book *The Seven Decisions*, he talks about creating your own personal board of directors, a group of people you surround yourself with who have the expertise in areas in which you need help. Your best friend may be a really good father who is willing to mentor you on parenting. Your financial advisor is the person you go to for financial advice. You may have a personal trainer who helps you with a diet and exercise plan. Even if you don't hire people to fill these roles, you can find people with whom you are friends to serve as unofficial mentors. What Andrews calls "Your Personal Board of Directors," we call "Your Dream Team."

Life can be complicated, with many moving parts that must be managed to live your Ultimate Life. No one was born with the wisdom to effectively manage career, marriage, family, finances, and health. We all need help, and we are surrounded by people with information and knowledge that can make a difference in our lives. Our good friend and business partner, Mitchell Schlimer has termed this *OPE,* or *Other People's Experiences.* We must leverage the experiences and knowledge of others as a foundation and launching point for the lives of our dreams.

Step 6: Always Seek Synergies

Walt Disney is considered one of the finest producers in the entertainment industry. It can be argued that no one has achieved his level of success and pushed an industry further. From the first film with synchronized sound to Disney World, his life embodied dreaming big and doing the impossible. For the first half of his career, Walt made a living producing films for movie theatres. When TV was introduced, it was a real threat to his livelihood. As a matter of fact, all the major film studios fought the new medium vehemently.

Walt Disney, however, sought to embrace television. He once said, "TV was not the enemy of the studios, but rather the ally." For him it became another way to distribute his products. What many people do not realize is that it was TV that actually enabled Walt to build Disneyland in California. At the time, ABC was the smallest of the three networks, lagging behind NBC and CBS. ABC was looking for new content that could reposition them and put them on a path of growth. Walt structured a deal to bring Disney programming to ABC, and gained an investment from them that actually allowed Disneyland to be constructed. The rest, as they say, is history. Moreover, the Disney brand and its famous front men, Walt Disney and Mickey Mouse, received critical exposure through television that propelled them into becoming one of the most powerful brands in the world today.

In his book, *The 21 Irrefutable Laws of Leadership*, John Maxwell describes a period of great stress in the life of John Schnatter, the founder of Papa John's Pizza. Schnatter had grown Papa John's to a fairly large pizza delivery business, but his life was a mess. He was stressed out and working ridiculous hours. In a cold sweat, Schnatter woke one morning with a clear realization. He concluded that he was unable to work any harder or any smarter than he was already working. Until he learned to work through others, his life would always be drastically limited. He changed his entire management philosophy, letting go of control, and empowering others to help him build the business. Today, Papa John's operates 3500 restaurants in all 50 states and in 29 countries.

Everyone who comes into your life can help you live your dreams. But it's up to you to find the synergy to apply it and create a better life for yourself, ultimately helping to make a better world. It's essential that you learn to effectively work with, for, and through others, because they can give you new knowledge and opportunities, provide you with critical talents and skills, and have an exponentially positive impact on the meaning of your life.

Step 7: Seek to Serve First

Zig Ziglar, author, businessman, and motivational speaker, is famous for saying, "You can get everything you want out of life, if you simply help enough others get what they want." As it relates to the *We Are Connected* mindset, no truer words have ever been spoken. As previously mentioned, almost all new knowledge and opportunities come through other people. So the question is, how do we best tap into those opportunities? The simple answer is to figure out what you can do to help them.

Remember, everyone who comes into your life can help you live your dreams. You must seek out this opportunity, and the best way to do so is to ask how *you* can help *them*. Create a dialogue that searches for the synergies in your new or expanding relationship. Once these synergies are found, the process of co-creation is maximized.

"Alone we can do so little; together we can do so much."

-Helen Keller

Mindset in A Minute

We Are Connected

Explore the synergies in all relationships and learn to empower one another.

Step 1. Create a Sense of Connectedness: The first step is to feel a sense of interconnectedness with others. This provides the foundation to build meaningful and synergistic relationships.

Step 2. Choose empowering relationships: Seek friendships and work associates with the intention of helping each other live lives of greater meaning and significance.

Step 3. Relish Competition: Get excited by competition, knowing that its primary purpose is to heighten your own performance and drive you to become better.

Step 4. Celebrate Diversity: Be proud of your unique genius, but also find beauty in those of all people. Understand the incredible contributions that people who are different from you can offer.

Step 5. Build Your Dream Team: Recognize all the people in your life that you can tap into for the guidance and support you need to maximize your potential and live your dreams.

Step 6. Always Seek Synergies: Actively seek synergies with everyone you meet, finding how you are able to assist and leverage one another to collective new heights.

Step 7. Seek to Serve First: Jumpstart all relationships by focusing first on what you can give or do to help others.

"The most important single ingredient in the formula of success is knowing how to get along with people."

-President Theodore Roosevelt

Chapter 6

100% Accountable

"If it is to be, it is up to me."

- William H. Johnsen

Do You Believe In Magic?

Earvin "Magic" Johnson is considered one of the greatest basketball players to ever play the game. Many experts also believe he was the game's finest point guard. His ability to pass the ball and involve his teammates was unparalleled, and, more importantly, that ability helped his team to succeed. Over the course of his career, his 10,141 assists earned him the number four spot in the basketball record book. However, even though his career was shortened due to illness, his average of 11.2 assists per game continues to rank number one and positions him as the best passer of all time.

In one game, with seconds left on the clock, Magic made a pass to a rookie teammate who was unable to catch the ball and fumbled it out of bounds. They lost the game. When interviewed after the game, Magic was asked about the pass and if he was frustrated that the young player was unable to catch it and make the basket. Magic's response was that it was a bad pass. The interviewer challenged him by saying it was perfect, the ball hit the player in the hands, and there was no reason he should have dropped it. Magic simply said, "Any pass I make that is not caught is a bad pass." He went on to explain that he knew the young player was nervous, and he was not mentally ready to catch the hard pass under all that pressure. Magic said under those circumstances he should have taken the shot himself.

Magic Johnson's thought process embodies the *100% Accountable* Mindset. Certainly, the rookie should have caught the pass, but the only thing Magic could have done to prevent the ball from being dropped was not to pass the ball to him in the first place. He could have easily placed the blame on his teammate and assumed the role of victim, as the vast majority of players would have done. Instead, he decided on accountability, and assessed what he needed to do differently the next time. Magic chose to learn and evolve, and that is a large reason why he is arguably the greatest point guard in the history of basketball.

The Counter Mindsets

Have you heard people say, "just my luck" when something doesn't go their way? How about, "I'd rather be lucky than good." Buying into these perspectives can be very dangerous. Unfortunately, many people walk around feeling like they have very little control over the circumstances in their life. From a mindset perspective, this can lead to a *victim* mentality. Once we start blaming other people and events for our situations in life, we become more likely to stop looking for ways to improve and change our future outcomes. For many people, this leads to getting stuck in a rut and repeating the same set of circumstances over and over again. This validates what Albert Einstein once said: "Insanity is doing the same thing over and over and expecting different results."

Once we stop looking in the mirror for the change, we lose control and become a victim of our own doing. We lack the perspective of

Lucius Annaeus Seneca, who once said, "Luck is what happens when preparation meets opportunity." This is the mindset people of profound happiness and success buy into. The ultra-successful understand that they may not be able to control all the events in their life, but they can control how they react to them. They also understand that how they react to events influences what happens next. When you fully embrace this mindset, the effects can be very liberating. You learn to appreciate that only you control the keys to your happiness and success. By following the suggested Mindsets in Action steps, you can move from victim to victor.

Mindset in Action: A Step By Step Approach

Step 1: Reconcile with the Past

In the movie *Forest Gump*, Gary Sinesc plays Lieutenant Dan, a bitter soldier who lost his legs in the Vietnam War. In the years following the war, Lieutenant Dan is very angry and highly focused on the unfairness of his disability. He becomes an alcoholic and watches his life unravel as he spirals out of control. In one scene, while on a shrimp boat stuck in a hurricane, Dan climbs to the highest mast on the ship and fights the hurricane with all his bitterness and anger. The next day, when the hurricane has passed, Forrest Gump finds Dan swimming in the water at complete peace. Somehow, during the night, he had fought off all his demons and reconciled with all the past transgressions against him. Lieutenant Dan was now prepared to move forward with his life. He decided to get artificial limbs and marry a woman from Vietnam. He reconciled his past and removed the mental baggage holding him back.

There is a Buddhist saying that illustrates this point: "Pain is inevitable, but suffering is optional." The problem most of us have when bad things occur is that we continue to relive them over and over again. They take over our lives, they make us bitter, and they channel all our energy away from what we need to do to achieve the happiness and success we all want. It's extremely hard for us to let go of anger, but we must realize that it's only hurting us, and find a way to reconcile and free ourselves from the past so we can effectively move forward. Remember that forgiveness begins and ends with yourself, and the pain you feel is only hurting you.

Step 2: Overcome Fears

Susan Jeffers is a bestselling author, self-help guru, and motivational speaker. In her book, *Feel the Fear and Do It Anyway*, she compares the alternatives of failing to a lack of action. In her assessment, the lack of action is exponentially more damaging than failure. Lack of action in the face of fears leads to incomplete and unfulfilled experiences and accomplishments, perhaps the greatest tragedy of all. People of success and happiness, she argues, muster the strength to face their doubts head on, and take action in the face of them.

Franklin D. Roosevelt once said "The only thing we have to fear is fear itself." Whether it is the fear of failure, abandonment, public speaking, or heights, the resulting non-action is most destructive. Alternatively, overcoming our fears is among the most exhilarating and empowering experiences we can ever have. Many of our students have a fear of public speaking. It is easy to understand how the inability to get up and communicate thoughts can limit one's future. People who fear abandonment are unable to enter into meaningful and positive relationships. We must recognize the destructive nature of our fears. We must seek to overcome short-term discomfort for the sake of the long-term realization of our dreams.

Step 3: Remove Limiting Beliefs

Have you ever felt like 24 hours is not enough time to get to all of the things you need to get done in a day? We are all very busy people. Whether you're raising a family, running a business, going to school, working one or more jobs, or all of the above, time is a precious commodity. We have kids who are very active in school, after school, and on the weekends. We run a large and growing global education company. We founded the Magic Wand Foundation, a non-profit organization dedicated to empowering youth. We go to the gym, stay involved in the community, walk our dogs, take our wives on dates, and find the time to read and try to improve ourselves. It's easy for us to run out of time and feel like there aren't enough hours in the day to do it all and do it well. But we've studied the ultra-successful, and have determined that each one of them also had the same 24-hour days and 365-day years that we have. A lack of time is simply an excuse we make to rationalize areas where we feel we are coming up short.

Dr. Wayne Dyer is one of the most notable bestselling authors and personal coaches in the world today. In his book, *Excuses Begone*, he discusses the limiting effect excuses have in our lives. Excuses, like fears, give us a reason to not do something, and when we do nothing, we all know what the results are. Some excuses might include "people can't change," "my situation is special," or "I'll do it tomorrow." As you can see, all of these prevent us from taking action, and new and purposeful action is the only way to alter our current path.

In addition to limiting beliefs, we all have thoughts that drain our energy and take us off our game. Anger, jealousy, and self-doubt are only a few of the emotions that divert our focus from what's really important in our lives. While it's unrealistic to remove all negative thoughts and emotions, it is critical that we learn to manage them and gain a higher level of control so we can maximize our potential. The *Sedona Method*, authored by Hale Dwoskins, is a powerful process that focuses on taking greater control of your thinking and channeling it toward more constructive things. NLP, or neurolinguistic programming, is another excellent approach to begin taking control of your limiting thoughts and beliefs. Do whatever works for you to start putting excuses in your rearview mirror.

Step 4: Accept Ownership of Your Results

John Wooden is considered one of the greatest coaches ever to coach any sport. He was named Coach of the Year six times. His UCLA Bruins Basketball team won 10 national championships over a 12-year period, including 7 years in a row, and had a long-standing record of 88 straight victories. Bill Walton, their remarkable center, once recounted an episode when UCLA was handed a rare loss. As the team went into the locker room, the finger of blame was being pointed in many different directions. The coaches had a bad game plan, the guards had too many turnovers, and the big men got out-rebounded. The team was divided, and Wooden saw an important opportunity. He stood up and took complete blame for the loss. He got out-coached and a simple adjustment he didn't make would have meant victory rather than defeat. As the team took a breath, finally not worrying about taking the blame for the defeat, Wooden worked his magic. He pointed at Walton and asked him to explain what he could have done differently that would have changed the outcome of the game. Walton struggled for a minute, then came up with something that could have enabled victory. Each player who had played in the game proceeded to do the same, identifying how the loss was his fault.

As the locker room grew quiet, Wooden said, "Now we can all start the process of getting better." It was an epiphany for the players. They instantly realized that each of them was to blame, that every one of them could have done things differently that could have changed the outcome. That was something they could work on, something they could move forward with. Now the team was back to the process of getting better and controlling the outcomes of their lives. The result was that UCLA went on to win the national championship again that year.

John Wooden epitomizes the *100% Accountable* mindset, a recognition that you completely control everything that happens in your life. You are not a victim of your past, and your future has not been determined. You are what you decide you will be from this point and each moment going forward. You are the product of the decisions you make, and the actions you take.

One other important aspect of this mindset is *Entitlement vs. Empowerment*. The mental habit of *entitlement* is a byproduct of the victim mentality. It is a belief that someone or some group owes you something. As soon as you buy into this, you give away your power to produce and create results in your life, and you become dependent on others. People who have achieved success and lives of extraordinary happiness and meaning refuse to allow anyone else to dictate their happiness and success.

Step 5: Change What You Control

In his book, *The Success Principals*, Jack Canfield presents a classic formula for the attainment of results in one's life. The formula, Event + Response = Outcome (E + R = O), explains that our life is a series of events or circumstances to which we respond in some way. The combination of the events and our responses determines the outcomes or results of our lives.

The secret to changing the circumstances of your life lies in this simple formula. We have developed a new, slightly different model of the formula, which demonstrates the power you have to not only change the outcomes in your life, but also improve all future events and circumstances.

Event + Response = Outcome
- **Thoughts**
- **Plans**
- **Actions**

Our adjustment to this classic formula illustrates what we do control. These include the thoughts and emotions we have, the plans we make, and the actions we take. By adjusting these three elements, we can easily change the outcomes in our lives. Moreover, as we change the outcomes in our lives, putting them on a path of greater positivity, we begin to see a shift in the future events or circumstances of our lives. The result is a cycle of positive change, created simply by how we respond to the events we experience.

We can change our lives by changing the way we do things in the present. Every action we take has an equal and opposite reaction. If we change what we do, we will change who we become.

An essential part of putting this life-changing formula into practice is measurement; not in the form of spreadsheets or statistical analysis, but rather by simply recognizing the positive shift. Like all people, we need positive feedback and affirmation that what we are doing is working. We must learn to recognize the little shifts. When we work out, we should pay attention to the improvement in our body. When we eat healthier, we should pay attention to the sensation of feeling better. If we adjust our management style, we can begin to see how people are responding to us differently. The life changes we seek and the dreams we hold are enabled by thousands of tiny steps. We must recognize the incremental improvements in our life every step of the way.

Step 6: Become Truly Free

Viktor Frankl is truly one of the most extraordinary men of all time. In 1942, this respected psychologist, along with his new bride, mother, father, and brother were arrested by the Nazis in Vienna, Austria, and sent to a concentration camp. Frankl spent three years living in some of the worst conditions known to modern man. When Dr. Frankl's concentration camp was liberated in 1945, he learned that his family had not survived.

What he observed in the extermination camp became the source of his "Logo Therapy." He noticed that those who lived had one thing in common: they had chosen to live rather than die. He found that when everything else had been taken–friends, food, dignity, and health–the one thing their captors could not take was choice... the choice to live. According to Frankl, the last of man's inalienable rights was the right of individuals to choose how they would respond in any given situation. Frankl said, "Everything can be taken from a person but one thing, the last of human freedoms: to choose one's attitude in any set of circumstances, to choose one's own way."

Freedom is a word that has been passed down for generations. It is an idea linked to political or religious ideology. One definition of freedom is, 'A state in which someone is able to act and live as he or she chooses, without being subject to any undue restraint or restriction.'

We think of restraints or restrictions imposed on us as laws. What about the restrictions we place on ourselves? Every time we do something out of character that is influenced by someone else, we are in a form of bondage. We may act differently around friends, we may get nervous when people are watching, or we may not take action for fear of being rejected by someone else. Each of these is an example of giving away our freedom.

Frankl once said they could take everything away, they could strip him naked and starve him, but they would never get his pride, his thoughts, or his hope for the future. This is the essence of true freedom, unencumbered by the thoughts and opinions of others, in which our actions are intrinsic and of the greatest possible alignment with our dreams and who we are.

Mindset in A Minute

100% Accountable

Choose to be responsible for your own happiness and success.

Step 1. Reconcile with the past: Find a way to free yourself from issues in your past. Remember that forgiveness begins and ends with you.

Step 2. Overcome fears: Recognize the destructive nature of your fears and take action, one step at a time, and you will start to experience the exhilaration of a breakthrough.

Step 3. Remove limiting beliefs: Realize that most limiting beliefs are self-imposed and have no truth or validity. Try exchanging your limiting belief for the exact opposite positive thought.

Step 4. Accept ownership of your results: The process for self-improvement begins when you take complete ownership of your current situation. When you stand in the truth, you give yourself permission to grow.

Step 5. Change what you control: While you may not control all of the circumstances in your life, you do control how you react to them. Your thoughts, emotions and actions influence your future outcomes.

Step 6. Become truly free: Recognize that true freedom resides inside of you, and, regardless of circumstances, you control your own attitude. This is also a great reminder that you should not waste energy trying to control another person's life, but rather, allow them the freedom of their own choices.

"If not now, when? If not here, where? If not me, who?"

-Steve Geiger

Chapter 7

Attitude of Gratitude

If you change the way you look at things, the things you look at change.

-Wayne Dyer

Penny for your thoughts?

It's estimated that approximately 65,000 thoughts go through our minds every day. About 95% of these thoughts are the exact thoughts we had the day before and the day before that. What's on our mind basically stays on our mind. This wouldn't be so bad, except that about 80% of our thoughts are fueled by negativity. The term to describe this is *Automatic Negative Thoughts*, or ANTs. We are people of habit, so when the same negative thoughts repeat each day, we become conditioned to believe them, regardless of how pessimistic they are. Our brains keep serving us negative thoughts all day, every day, and for the majority of people, it hasn't been a fair fight... until now.

Best-selling author and leadership expert John Maxwell describes an interesting research study on professional athletes in his book, *Talent is Never Enough*. According to Maxwell, pro athletes have 25% fewer thoughts each day than the average person. This by no means implies that they have fewer intellectual thoughts, just fewer negative thoughts. Their secret holds the key to positive change for the rest of us. It begins with the pros' understanding of how powerfully their thoughts affect their daily performance. Every day, they miss shots, throw interceptions, strike out, make bad plays and lose games. They don't want these negative memories to haunt them, so they use techniques to eliminate them and keep them from repeating every day. They simply have fewer negative thoughts, and it improves their performance. We will teach you some of these techniques so you can put them to work in your life.

It's fairly easy for most of us to be grateful for the good things in our lives. According to Martin Seligman's global research project on happiness, that's good news, because systematically being grateful can increase our lifespan. Seligman, the father of the positive psychology movement, has performed extensive studies on the impact of gratitude on our life experience. In one study, he tested people who were depressed. Each person was asked to spend a few minutes each day writing down the things for which they were grateful. The results were amazing. 92% felt happier, 94% were less depressed, 84% felt less stressed, and 78% had more energy. Even more amazing, the study estimated that by simply expressing daily gratitude, we can add 6.9 years to our lives; that's an impact superior to quitting smoking or performing regular exercise. Our research revealed several techniques for increasing gratitude in your daily life, and we will share them with you shortly.

However, there was one significant finding that we didn't expect. An *Attitude of Gratitude* extends far beyond the typical things for which people tend to be thankful. In fact, the unexpected blueprint for an extraordinary life includes being grateful for your challenging situations too.

The Counter Mindsets

A study was performed that asked people about their experience in the subway. The participants were asked what percentage of the time the train going in the opposite direction they were traveling came before the train for which they were waiting. The overwhelming majority of travelers believed the other train came first more often. The truth of the matter is that the statistics showed both trains came first 50% of the time. Termed the "Subway Fallacy," this study demonstrates a collective condition of our society. The anger and frustration created by the other train coming first created a more memorable experience. When the traveler's train came first, it created no indelible image or memory in their mind. They can recall more of the negative experiences, hence the perception that the other train came more often. Unfortunately, we live in a world that is being conditioned more by negative experiences than positive ones.

In his book *Authentic Happiness*, Martin Seligman shares research that indicates depression is 10 times more prevalent today than it was in 1960. Unfortunately, it is also affecting much younger people: the average age has gone from 29.8 to 14.5 years old, and it has very little to do with money. Seligman's study shows that once household income reaches $8,000 per year per person; there is no correlation between an amount of money and happiness. As a matter of fact, real income in the US has increased by 16% over the last 30 years, while the number of people describing themselves as happy has decreased from 36% to 29%.

Somehow, in the fast-paced world of today, we've lost sight of what matters most and are no longer connected to the things that build meaning and happiness in our lives. The more we get, the more we realize what we do not have, and so we're constantly seeking more and more. Our energy is focused on what we don't have and on what's missing. The Mindsets in Action steps below will help you incorporate the *Attitude of Gratitude* mindset into your daily life.

Mindset in Action: A Step By Step Approach

Step 1: Focus on the Positives

Martin Seligman believes that more than 98% of psychologists make their money focusing on problems. His movement went against the grain, seeking ways to build from a foundation of positivity so that our children could become immune to the many social and emotional problems we face today. There is a quote that says, "Energy flows where attention goes." The things we focus our attention on are the things that expand in our life. Many people focus their attention on what they don't have, or on what they have and don't want. As long as their minds are focused on this lack, these challenges will persist and likely expand in their life. Seligman is begging us to use the positives as the foundation of our lives.

A very common practice used by marriage counselors epitomizes the "focus on the positives" mentality. Typically, what happens in struggling marriages is a focus on what isn't working and each other's character flaws or personality deficiencies. When the attention goes to the negatives, that is where the energy of the relationship flows. Experts like Denis Waitley, Wayne Dyer, and Deepak Chopra describe a simple strategy that's been used by psychologists for many years. Simply stated, psychologists ask couples to write down all the things they like about the other person, and then instruct them to focus more and more on those things. What often happens next transforms marriages. The two begin seeing each other in a different light, and more often find themselves in situations where the other is in his or her element. Both of their demeanors change, and a new positive energy comes to inhabit the relationship. By adjusting the focus of their attention, they begin enjoying far more positive results and feelings in their relationship.

When your mind is focused on scarcity and lack, it is impossible to begin leveraging your assets to build the life of your dreams. We have two choices in life: we can elect to focus on the negatives, or we can choose to build on all the positive things. If you choose the negatives, you risk living in a downward spiral. If you build from the positives, there is nowhere to go but up.

Step 2: Journal Your Gratitude

Oprah Winfrey is well known for keeping a daily gratitude journal, a practice she was taught by her mentor, Maya Angelou. As Oprah put it:

> *"I live in the space of thankfulness, and I have been rewarded a million times over for it. I started out giving thanks for small things, and the more thankful I became, the more my bounty increased. That's because what you focus on expands, and when you focus on the goodness in your life, you create more of it. Opportunities, relationships, even money flowed my way when I learned to be grateful no matter what happened in my life."*

The *Attitude of Gratitude* is not a one-time project, nor is it a series of incremental steps. It is a way of life that infuses energy into every aspect of your being. Napoleon Hill coined it *PMA*, or *Positive Mental Attitude*. It was the defining characteristic of people like Walt Disney, Dale Carnegie, and Norman Vincent Peale. Simply stated, a PMA causes you to expect more from each moment, and because of this, you extract more out of your time.

We suggest you keep a daily gratitude journal. In your journal, write down the obvious things for which you are grateful. This might include your health, family, and friends. Also include often-overlooked items such as the air you breathe, the water you drink, or even a beautiful flower. As Martin Seligman pointed out, keeping a daily journal of that for which you're grateful can even increase your lifespan. To really boost gratitude in your life, we would also suggest that you pay attention to the good things that happen to you each day, simply making a mental note of each event in your mind. Our research demonstrates that, at a minimum, you will feel happier with what you have, which can make all the difference in the world.

Step 3: Defuse the Negatives

Have you ever had one of those days that starts off wrong and seems to get worse and worse? Perhaps you oversleep and then stub your toe on the way to the bathroom. Maybe some toothpaste gets on your shirt and you have to change your clothes. Throughout the day, one misstep feeds into another. It doesn't take long for you to start stringing together one bad day after another, and then one bad week becomes a bad month and so on. This doesn't mean that everything that happens is bad, but it starts to feel like you might be in a rut. You may even feel like you're a magnet for misfortune. If you've ever felt like this, don't worry, because you aren't alone. Here's a technique you can use to defuse the negatives before they pile on. It's based on a process Scott developed and teaches to thousands of students. He explains:

When I was a little boy, I was afraid of the dark. I needed a night light just to help me go to sleep. To this day, when I walk into a dark room I feel a bit uneasy. As soon as I flip the switch and the lights come on, I feel much better. Just like walking into a dark room and turning the light switch on, I've learned to flip my emotional switch from negative to positive. I imagine I have an invisible light switch on my chest right on top of my heart. When I feel uneasy because a negative thought or emotion enters my stream of consciousness (one of those daily ANTs), I pretend to flip my imaginary switch from negative to positive. Basically, when I flip the switch, I stop giving any thought or emotion to what I don't want, and replace what I'm thinking and feeling with something positive. Sometimes it's the exact opposite thought, and sometimes it's a completely different thought, as long as it's one that is purely positive.

Step 4: Thank it Forward

Do you remember the movie *Pay it Forward*? It came out in 2000, and the concept was so innovative that a national foundation called the Pay it Forward Foundation was created. The idea is that to change the world, all you need to do is a favor for a few people with no expectation of being paid back. Instead, you ask those people to kindly pay it forward by doing three random favors for other people. Exponentially, these random acts of kindness can change the world for the better. Random acts of kindness are a great way to increase the level of gratitude you experience. It just feels great to do something nice for someone else with no expectation of anything in return. Our research demonstrated that the ultra-successful believe that when they do a good deed, it comes back to them many times over.

Here's one more technique you might want to try. This was developed by one of our good friends, Christopher Koke. He suggests you seek out people to say 'thank you' to each day. Saying thank you and meaning it is free and, therefore, not in limited supply. Often, the people closest to us, our family and friends, hear it the least. It's socially expected to thank our customers, vendors, and even colleagues for the obvious. Chris is suggesting something much deeper. He's talking about saying thank you on a really personal level. Be on the hunt for things for which you can be thankful, and this will help redirect you from the typical list of things you wish would change. By focusing on gratitude and giving thanks, you will soon find that you have even more for which to be grateful. Chris also suggests, for a truly energizing experience, to consider adding a hug when appropriate. When you openly express thanks, you physically feel great. When another person receives an authentic thank you, they also feel good. This one is a real win-win.

Step 5: See Both Sides of the Coin

Scott says:

Every now and then I have a silly argument with my wife over the temperature in our house. I say it's hot in here and she says it's cold. Then I walk over to the thermostat to prove my point. I read it aloud and tell her it's a hot 70 degrees. Her reply is usually, 'that's exactly what I said, it's cold in here.' Then we argue whether 70 degrees is hot or cold. It's so silly, but we both tend to get worked up over it. After twenty years of marriage, these are not our best moments. So is it hot or is it cold? The answer is... it just is. It's just 70 degrees. In this case, 70 degrees represents two sides of a coin. For me, it's hot, and for my wife it's cold.

While this may seem like an insignificant thing to bring up, our research shows us that happy people tend to argue less often. They find ways to get along with others. They seek peaceful resolutions, and one way they accomplish this is by appreciating and accepting that other people have their own perspectives. As Dr. Phil McGraw, best-selling author of *Life Strategies,* says, "Even a flattened pancake has two sides." Learn to appreciate and acknowledge the views of others without having to prove your perspective as "right," and you will significantly increase your happiness factor.

Step 6: Become an Inverse Paranoid

Tony Robbins has successfully coached millions of people, including a number of presidents. He often describes the time in his life when his father left him and his family: One Thanksgiving, a man came to the door offering Tony's family some food. Tony's father was jobless, and the family was struggling. Tony's father was ashamed and became very angry, demanding the man leave and never come back. Later that night, Tony's father walked out the door and abandoned his family forever. At the time, it was the worst day of Tony's life.

As Robbins looks back on that day when a stranger made a charitable gift of food, he realized that it was the first time he understood that other people really did care about him and his family. When Tony was a bit older and his family was finally out of poverty's grip, he began giving food away every Thanksgiving. He would put the food by the door, ring the doorbell, and run away. He says those are some of the most powerful experiences of his life. Today, Tony has a foundation that feeds millions of people every year during Thanksgiving and Christmas.

On reflection, Tony considers the day his father left to be among the best days of his life. Instead of living a life fueled by emptiness, he started living a life filled with gratitude. The new gratitude he felt came from understanding that he was part of an amazing family of people whose lives are so full of joy and happiness that it flows out from them and into the lives of others, filling them like empty vessels. Once those vessels are full, they overflow, and the cycle of gratitude continues.

The term *Inverse Paranoid* was coined by W. Clement Stone, a businessman and philanthropist. The essential meaning of the term was handed down to people like Jack Canfield and Mark Victor Hansen of *Chicken Soup for the Soul* fame. Keep in mind, classic paranoia is described as the belief that the world and all in it are out to get you. Inverse Paranoids, on the other hand, truly believe some invisible force is constantly working for them, and not against them. They are vigilant in taking the good from all situations and using it in building toward their ultimate success.

We often asked the people we interviewed about defining moments in their lives—the moment or time they believed was the catalyst to their success. Invariably, they mentioned a time of true adversity and challenge, and pointed to a character trait that was developed or a knowledge that was gained. Talk to anyone of great success, and they will always point to the moments of adversity in their life as the catalyst for their accomplishments. It is in the times of substantial challenge that character is built, knowledge is attained, and creativity is heightened.

Likewise, consider the things in your life that may not seem so positive. Become an Inverse Paranoid, and identify how those things will ultimately benefit you, possibly by teaching you a lesson or giving you a new perspective. When you experience challenging situations in life, especially serious tragedies, it's only human to feel loss, sorrow and even suffering. We hope you can find solace in the fact that it will only be a matter of time before you can look back with a greater sense of clarity on the situation. Perhaps your worst day will somehow become your best day.

"Keep your face to the sunshine, and you cannot see a shadow."

-Helen Keller

Mindset in A Minute

Attitude of Gratitude

Seek the positives from every experience and be thankful for all you have.

Step 1. Focus on the Positives: Choose to use the positive things in your life as the foundation. Utilize the saying "energy flows where attention goes," focus on the positives, and allow those to be the things that expand in your life.

Step 2. Journal your gratitude: Constantly recognize the good things that happen in your life. Pay attention to and record the positive things that happen to you each day.

Step 3. Defuse the negatives: Learn to dismiss the ANT's (automatic negative thoughts) by flipping the switch from negative thoughts and emotions to positive ones.

Step 4. Thank it forward: Make time to thank people in your life for big and small things, and look to perform random acts of kindness.

Step 5. See both sides of the coin: Understand that each person has their own unique perspective, and learn to accept and appreciate their opinion without having to prove yourself right. Work to not judge things as good or bad, right or wrong. Accept everything that happens as a wonderful, natural unfolding of your life and dreams.

Step 6. Become an Inverse Paranoid: Like the most successful people, learn to expect that good things will happen to you. Assume the universe is conspiring to do you good; even when things feel negative, understand that good will come from it and seek it out.

"Life is not about waiting for the storms to pass... it's about learning how to dance in the rain."

-Vivian Greene

Chapter 8

Live to Give

We make a living by what we get, we make a life by what we give.
                                                            -Winston Churchill

A Social Adventure

People of achievement and happiness get more out of life because they give more. The vast majority of society believes in one of two paths. Either you achieve a certain level of financial means and then start giving to charity, or you give first, sowing the seeds along your journey. Our research found many examples of people in both categories, just as we anticipated. What we didn't expect was a much deeper meaning and execution of what we call the *Live to Give* mindset. For starters, the concept of giving, in the world of the ultra-successful, is most accurately defined as giving your best life to the world. In other words, being the best You possible. In their best-selling book, *The Go-Givers*, authors Bob Burg and John David Mann describe this principle as "The Law of Authenticity," stating, "The most valuable gift you have to offer is yourself."

Interestingly, the way the people we researched have been able to live their best lives is by thoroughly embracing the *Passion First* mindset. Because they are aligned with their authentic passions and strengths, they execute their lives better; they accomplish more, and consequently give more to the world around them. Quite simply, they create more value.

We create value in this world when we do things that are positive and constructive. When we create value, we have an impact. When our actions are positive and purposeful, the impact we have on ourselves and on others is beneficial. The beauty of the *Live to Give* mindset is that we get what we give. Science teaches us that every action has an equal and opposite reaction, and that the energy we give off never dies, it only changes forms. When we create positive value in the world, the world responds in kind. We are usually compensated in the form of monetary income, but often the currency that has greater value is psychic income or a feeling of significance. When we live our best life, striving toward our fullest potential, we feel a greater sense of worth, accomplishment, and positive impact. This alone increases our sense of happiness, joy and fulfillment. It would almost appear to be selfish if it were not for the amazing side effects. When we give all that we can possibly give, the world is a better place.

Consider Martin Luther King Jr., endowed with tremendous charisma and the ability to inspire, who aligned his abilities around the causes of equality and fighting segregation. The alignment of his unique abilities within the context of his life propelled him to a life of meaning, and afforded him the opportunity to make extraordinary contributions to the world. The same can be said of Mother Teresa, Nelson Mandela, and Mahatma Gandhi. Lives of great meaning are led from an orientation toward service, and the sharing of oneself to the advantage of others.

There is one final observation that seems to be a game changer in the land of extraordinary living. When people connect their passion to causes they believe in, the multiplier effect on their contributions to society is off the charts. We're not talking about surface giving, like when businesses donate a small percentage of their profits to charity. We're not knocking that by any means, but there seems to be an entirely different level of living to give when businesses are built around doing well while doing good.

The late Anita Roddick was one of our interview subjects who clearly fit this description. At 33 years old, Roddick was a housewife who opened a store in Brighton, England, to support herself and her two children. She barely had enough money for the rent. What she did have was a passion for environmentally friendly products, fair trade, and a host of other social causes she actively and openly supported through in-store signs and significant donations. She was a leader in social responsibility before most even knew what that meant. She turned the tables on social responsibility and made it into more of a social adventure as she grew her tiny store, The Body Shop, into more than 1,000 retail locations in over 40 countries. Wanting to make the point that anyone, from practically any means, can make a difference, Anita shared this off-the-cuff quote: "If you think you're too small to have an impact, try going to bed with a mosquito in the room."

The Counter Mindsets

Does charity begin at home? Can we only give our money and time when we have more of both? Is our work about making a living? These are very rational and practical questions. Is it possible that saving our good graces for ourselves and our families is limiting our lives? Could it be possible that the best way to earn more money and time is to give them both first? These may seem like counterintuitive concepts, but our research demonstrates that the ultra-successful seem to experience a different reality.

In his book, *The 7 Spiritual Laws of Success*, Deepak Chopra says that the universe has a perfect accounting system. His point is simply that we get out of life exactly what we give, every single time. Most of us live in a world imprisoned by the perception of scarcity. We must get *ours* because there is not enough to go around. We often ask, "What's in it for me?" It is this mentality that cuts off the flow of abundance in our lives. We shut off the connections to so many new opportunities that come through the process of giving and sharing of oneself. We drastically limit the value we create, which in turn decreases the value we receive.

We get paid for the work we do, yet many of us are left wanting more. You get out of relationships what you put into them, yet most of us seek deeper meaning and connections. We are what we eat, yet most people desire greater health and wellness. Everything we are and ever will be is a product of the things we do to attain them. We must do more to get more, because the universe may truly have a perfect accounting system.

And what about the work we do? We must re-orient how we perceive that as well. Today, one of the strongest measures of job quality is salary. Most of us seek employment with the hope of getting the highest financial return for the work we do. As discussed in the *Passion First* chapter, this can ultimately act in direct opposition to success, happiness, and even financial return. We must seek employment that provides us the greatest opportunity to serve, create value, and maximize our positive impact. When we do this, we create more value, and as a result, more value is showered upon us. Giving of our time, talent, and treasure does not need to feel like a responsibility, but rather an opportunity with an incredible return on investment: an extraordinary life!

Mindset in Action: A Step By Step Approach

Step 1: Share Your Unique Genius

Nature teaches us many lessons, and none as profound as the true essence of service. Consider an oak tree. The best thing an oak tree can do is grow to its fullest potential. The larger its size, the more shade it provides, the more leaves it drops that nourish the soil, the more acorns to feed the animals, and the more life-giving oxygen it produces for the surrounding habitat. The seemingly selfish act of feeding itself with sunlight and soil nutrients empowers the oak to do the most good, not only for itself, but also for the world around it.

Bill Gates has donated billions of dollars to charity. All of this money is going toward wonderful causes that are benefitting millions if not billions of people. However, no amount of money donated by Gates will equal the impact Gates has had through the creation of Microsoft, and the software revolution he helped drive. Oprah, like Gates, is a generous philanthropist. That being said, the impact Oprah has had on improving the lives of millions of people through her talk show and other media outlets will never be equaled through her charitable giving.

The greatest contribution any of us can ever make for our family, community, and the world is simply to achieve our maximum potential. When we find our unique genius and align it with the world around us, we maximize our positive impact. We accomplish more, and we ultimately get more in return.

Step 2: Give Before You Get

Blake Mycoskie is an entrepreneur and the founder of TOMS Shoes. In 1996, he took a trip to Argentina, where he became interested in a rope-soled shoe that Argentinean farmers had been wearing for over 100 years. Not only did Blake notice these unusual shoes, he also couldn't help but notice how many people, mostly children, were shoeless. He learned that because so many people couldn't afford shoes, they had no choice but to go barefoot. Being shoeless increased their risk of life-threatening diseases caused by bacteria in the soil entering the body through cuts and scrapes on the feet. Around the world, more than 300 million children are shoeless. Over one million children die each year from preventable diseases, simply because they have no shoes. Millions more don't attend school because they can't meet the basic dress code or sustain the journey to travel to school without footwear.

TOMS shoes was created with a new business model based on a one-for-one principle. For every pair of shoes TOMS sells, one pair is donated to a child in need. After selling 10,000 pairs of shoes from his apartment, Blake returned to Argentina with friends, loved ones, and his new TOMS Family to hand-deliver 10,000 pairs of shoes to kids in need. Following his success in Argentina, Blake went to South Africa, where he hand-delivered 50,000 pairs of shoes to children. Since its founding, TOMS has donated more than 1 million pairs of shoes to children around the world. Recently, TOMS introduced a new product, sunglasses, with the same one-for-one model. For every pair of sunglasses sold, they provide sight-giving cataract surgery to someone in need.

When Napoleon Hill studied the most successful men and women in the history of the United States, he found a number of unifying qualities that separated them from the masses. In *Think and Grow Rich,* he stated that one of those qualities was, "They give before they get." In other words, the best way to start the flow of abundance in your life is to begin the process of giving and serving others. Blake has been able to grow his for-profit business faster than most shoe companies, in spite of the fact that he has no advertising budget. The initial advice he received from consultants was to first establish a financially sound business, and then begin donating shoes. While this made rational sense, Blake opted to give first and right from the very beginning.

Step 3: Seek Ways to Serve

Harris Rosen grew up in the Lower Eastside of New York City. His family was poor and barely scraped by. Harris learned to swim at the local Boys' Club, which provided programs and services to city kids in need. Nearly 60 years later, he still swims every day—only now he swims at one of the seven hotels he owns in Orlando, Florida. When we interviewed Harris, he spoke of how important it is to serve others. He mentioned that anyone could do it simply by being friendly and generous with his or her time. He reflects fondly on his days at the Boys' Club, citing that it was less about a place to swim and more about connecting with caring individuals who were genuinely concerned for his well-being. Today, Harris employs over 4,500 people, and has his own staff of doctors and nurses that provides onsite medical benefits for employees and their families. Perhaps this is the reason why he has one of the highest retention rates in the hospitality industry in his area. He also thinks it's one of the reasons his team goes out of their way when serving guests at any of the Rosen Hotels & Resorts. Service is contagious and, remarkably, both the giver and receiver feel a sense of empowerment.

Mr. Rosen is an amazing entrepreneur who lives the *7 Mindsets*. We learned why *Forbes* magazine named him one of the most generous philanthropists in America. Harris has adopted the disadvantaged community of Tangelo Park in Florida. He provides free pre-school for all of the two-, three-, and four-year-old children from the neighborhood. He also makes a promise to every young person from the community that if he or she graduates from high school and is accepted into a vocational school, community college, or four-year public university in Florida, he will pay the full tuition, room and board. To date, he has provided approximately 200 students with scholarships, and has plans to continue inspiring local students to reach new heights.

Each of us has opportunities to serve others every day, whether at work, at home, in school, or around the community. It begins with having a generous heart and recognizing that even the little things make a big difference. Lao Tzu once said, "He who gathers has little and he who scatters has much." The irony is that he who scatters gathers more. The best way to create abundance in your life is to start the cycle that begins with serving others.

Step 4: Align with Your Passions

Serving others can and should be one of the most inspiring and engaging activities in which we participate. We like to call it the social adventure of our lives. To live up to the motto, we must align who and what we serve with the activities and causes that matter to us. When we do this, it becomes highly relevant, it becomes exciting, and the objectives of the effort become critically important to us as individuals. As you might imagine, our chances of having more success and heightened meaning increase exponentially. Thus, we gain more meaning, and are much more likely to perform similar activities in the future.

If we look at philanthropists and achievers, their success is predicated on a cause that is of fundamental importance to them. For Mother Theresa, it was serving the impoverished people of India; for Gandhi, it was freeing the oppressed; and for Martin Luther King, Jr., it was ending segregation. It was the purpose that created the passion that drove the activity that accomplished the goal.

Look for ways to incorporate authentic giving in all you do. Connect your passion with a purpose larger than yourself. Whether through a business, a job, or volunteer work, aligning your passion with a *Live to Give* mindset will increase your sense of purpose, happiness, and positive impact on others.

"Do all the good you can, by all the means you can, in all the ways you can, in all the places you can, at all the times you can, to all the people you can, as long as ever you can."

-John Wesley

Mindset in A Minute

Live to Give

Inspire and serve others while you maximize your potential.

Step 1. Share your unique genius: Understand that the greatest contribution any of us can make is to leverage our unique talents, strengths, and passions, and share them with the world to the maximum extent possible.

Step 2. Give before you get: Know that the best way to get what you want in life is to give first. Once you start creating value for others, the world responds in kind with greater abundance in your life.

Step 3. Seek ways to serve: Incorporate the mentality of service in every aspect of your life. Understand the value of your life is the sum of the impacts you have. Seek to have the greatest possible positive impact in everything you do.

Step 4. Align with your passions: Make the benefits of what you do be of profound importance to who you are and the legacy you want to leave with your life. When you do this, you will invigorate everything you do, create greater value with your actions, and ultimately receive greater benefit in return.

A candle loses nothing by lighting another candle.

-Father James Keller

Chapter 9

The Time Is Now

"It is not the critic who counts: not the man who points out how the strong man stumbles or where the doer of deeds could have done better. The credit belongs to the man who is actually in the arena, whose face is marred by dust and sweat and blood, who strives valiantly, who errs and comes up short again and again, because there is no effort without error or shortcoming, but who knows the great enthusiasms, the great devotions, who spends himself for a worthy cause; who, at the best, knows, in the end, the triumph of high achievement, and who, at the worst, if he fails, at least he fails while daring greatly, so that his place shall never be with those cold and timid souls who knew neither victory nor defeat."

-President Theodore Roosevelt

An International Hero

Fred DeLuca is the founder of SUBWAY®, arguably one of the most successful restaurant franchises in the world. We interviewed Fred and discussed his book, *Start Small Finish Big*, to get his perspective on the nature of living big dreams. In his words, "You simply have to start by taking small steps." Subway is a classic example of a young man taking small but purposeful steps. Many of

DeLuca's early actions were ill-fated. On the opening day of his first restaurant, he only had one knife to cut the sandwiches. He wasn't prepared, the line of people became frustrated, and many left.

His first store didn't make a profit, and he thought about closing the business. He was conflicted, because he had a goal to open five sandwich shops within five years. He knew that if he closed this store, even if it was losing money, he would be moving in the opposite direction of his goal. Against the advice of others, he opened a second store, which also lost money. It took five years, five stores, and a significant amount of struggle before his concept started to work. Success for DeLuca came with time because he acted, he learned, and he adjusted. This is the process of success. Rarely does someone achieve greatness because of one magnificent moment. On the contrary, success is comprised of a thousand tiny but meaningful steps that ultimately result in dream realization. As Fred puts it, "Starting small is better than never starting at all."

"To achieve greatness, start where you are, use what you have, and do what you can."

-Arthur Ashe

The *Time Is Now* mindset delivers the power to activate your Ultimate Life and enjoy the journey every step of the way. Learning the 7 Mindsets and living them are two completely different things. You've probably heard the saying, "Knowledge is power," but it's the implementation of the knowledge that leads to the power. This isn't necessarily a revelation, but there does seem to be a significant difference in the level of action amongst the ultra-successful as compared to the average person. In our interview with Mark Victor Hansen, co-author of the *Chicken Soup for the Soul* series, he pointed out that there's a big gap between what people know and what they do. In this chapter, we will share with you our research-based findings on what you can do now to activate the mindsets in your daily life.

The Counter Mindsets

As well-intentioned as the saying, "Good things come to those who wait" may be, it has the potential to completely derail your dreams. So many people fail to reach their potential because they simply don't take enough action. Perhaps they hesitate because they are unsure of the path to take. Maybe it's fear that holds them back. Or it could be that they are waiting for others to join them or lead the way. What we do know is that far too many people end up settling in life, when the difference between ordinary and extraordinary can literally be one 'extra' step in the direction of their dreams.

There are two other memes we believe contribute to inactivity. We want to point these out, because freeing yourself from their grip can make all the difference. Growing up, we all became familiar with the saying "Don't make the same mistake twice." When parents say this, their intent is to teach children to learn from their mistakes and make the necessary adjustments to get it right the next time. When we ask students what this means to them, they tell us it has taught them that mistakes are bad. Unfortunately, that is a huge disconnect that does a great deal of harm.

How about the warning, "If it ain't broke, don't fix it"? Did you know that when Albert Einstein was a young man, most physicists believed that they knew everything there was to know about the workings of the universe? Luckily for us, Einstein didn't believe what other physicists believed, because he developed his theory of relativity and changed everything; now the world is a much different place.

We have conditioned acceptance into our culture. We are teaching ourselves not to challenge the status quo, and worse, we are not acting on our dreams and inspirations. Newton's law of motion says that every action has an equal and opposite reaction. Our failure to act manifests into a failure to get results. Learn to embrace *The Time Is Now* mindset, and you will experience a new world of possibilities.

"Take the first step in faith. You don't have to see the whole staircase, just take the first step."

-Dr. Martin Luther King, Jr.

Mindset in Action: A Step By Step Approach

Step 1: Enjoy Now

Eckhart Tolle is the bestselling author of *The Power of Now* and *The New Earth*. In his books, Tolle focuses on the concept of "presence," which simply translates into the ability to stay completely in the current moment. It is our ability to do this that galvanizes our effectiveness as individuals and increases the depth of meaning in our lives. Tolle would certainly agree with the quote by Bill Keane, "Yesterday is history, tomorrow is a mystery, but today is a gift... and that is why they call it the present."

Somehow, over the course of our lives, we have been desensitized to the amazing beauty and wonder that surround us. Claude Monet once said that if he could create the world on a blank canvas, he would be unable to create anything more beautiful and spectacular than what nature has created for us. From the colors of the rainbow, the air we take in, and the cool water we drink, life is truly a gift that we often take for granted.

If you think about it, the true measure of one's quality of life is the sum of the moments he or she spends on earth. Learn to find pleasure in the moment. Enjoy each and every moment as the singular and wonderful experience it is. Embrace the time and place you're in and the people you're with. To improve the quality of your life, find more meaning and joy in the now. Do this often enough, and you will begin stringing together more and more moments of peace and joy.

Step 2: Understand that Everything You Do Matters

The *Butterfly Effect* is a scientific concept based on the chaos theory. The namesake "Butterfly" comes from the notion that a butterfly flapping its wings in one part of the world could cause a hurricane on the other side. This scientific theory teaches us the incredibly interconnected nature of all things. It helps us understand how everything we do matters, not just to us, but to everyone and for all time.

Writer and speaker Andy Andrews expands on this concept when telling the story of Raymond Baker, who was given an award for hydrolyzing corn, a process credited with providing food for and saving over two billion lives in impoverished areas around the world. Andrews explains that Baker had been hired by Henry Wallace, Vice President of the United States under President Franklin D. Roosevelt, to run a lab to hydrolyze corn. Henry Wallace had been a protégé of George Washington Carver, who had instilled in Wallace a passion for agriculture and using his skills to solve major world issues. George Washington Carver's life had been saved by a young farmer named John Bentley, a stranger hired by Moses Carver to find George, his mother and brother, all of whom had been kidnapped by a team of raiders. George's mother was sold into slavery, and he never saw her again. Moses Carver and his wife raised Carver and his brother as their own sons and provided them with a first class education, something unheard of in Carver's time.

Andrews' point is that while Baker was credited with saving two billion lives, untold actions had been taken by others throughout history that set the stage for Baker to hydrolyze corn and save those lives. If Bentley had not saved Carver's life and put him on the road to greatness, then perhaps Baker would have never saved two billion lives—an example of the Butterfly Effect in action. Sir Isaac Newton once said, "If I have seen farther than others, it is because I have stood on the shoulders of giants." Andrews emphasizes that not only do our actions matter to us; they matter to everyone. Everything we do impacts our lives and sends ripples flowing outward forever. Nothing you do is insignificant.

Step 3: Get in the Zone

We had the opportunity to hear the Dalai Lama speak in Atlanta in 2010. He was asked what he felt about the United States, and what he thought was our deepest need. He simply stated that he wished more of us would seek to act from a place of warm-heartedness. What the Dalai Lama calls warm-heartedness is simply an expression of good feeling. It can be love, gratitude, empathy, compassion, or joy. It is when we are at our best and when the things we do have the greatest possible impact on the world around us.

Success is predicated on our ability to act from a position of strength. At the very core of this is how we feel at the time we perform the action. Parents know how much more effective they are when love or empathy is driving their action versus anger and frustration. Deepak Chopra once gave this simple advice to parents: "Be only love, and show only love." His meaning is simple. If our actions are driven by love, whether they are stern words of discipline or kind words of recognition, those actions will be positive and in the best interest of the child.

Perhaps the greatest things any of us can do are learn to manage our emotions, to understand when we are off our path, and rein in the negativity to avoid doing harm to ourselves or to others. With practice, you can learn to flip the switch and alter your emotions so that you act from a position of strength. Athletes call this place the *zone*, a state of heightened and often optimal performance. This is not a condition that should be reserved for athletes, but one you should learn to incorporate and recognize in your life on a regular basis. When you are feeling stressed or angry, you are not in the zone. Try taking a deep breath, relax, and tune into the zone before taking important action.

Step 4: Be a Continuous Learner

Michael Jordan took the game winning shot 51 times during the course of his college and professional career, but he missed 26 times. Babe Ruth is considered one of the greatest home run hitters, but he also led the league in strikeouts for 5 years, striking out 1330 times! That's almost twice the number of home runs he hit. The Wright Brothers were ridiculed during many of their failed attempts at flight. The point is that some of the most famed accomplishments of all time have been riddled with failure, yet very few people remember the failures; they remember the achievements.

We live in a world of cause and effect. To get a result, something must happen. That is simply a fact. To get results, we must act. We cannot get hung up on the past, and we can't afford to wait for everything to line up perfectly, because it never will. What often gets in the way is fear of failure and fear of the unknown. When we asked the ultra-successful what their impression of risk was, the overwhelming majority rarely saw anything they ever did as risky. They simply took action with expected outcomes, and when the outcomes were not what they expected, it became a learning experience from which they could grow and get better. They seem to have a certain comfort with ambiguity, and they prepare themselves to adjust the course of action as they gather new data.

Therein lie the fundamental ingredients to success: the constant initiative to take action, coupled with the inherent mentality to continually learn and adjust from the experience. What most people call failure, successful people call feedback. Ambrose Redmond once said, "Courage is not the absence of fear, but the ability to act in the face of it." Genius, then, comes from understanding that failure only occurs when you don't learn from it.

Step 5: Act on Purpose

Beck Weathers was part of an ill-fated Mt. Everest expedition that took place in May of 1996. On that day, the climbers got caught in a terrible storm at the top of the mountain that left eight dead, including two of the most experienced high altitude climbers in the world. Weathers lost the use of his eyes due to the effects of the high altitude. Buried in the snow, he was left for dead by some other climbers who had come upon him and believed him to have already died.

Jeff met Beck Weathers one evening when Weathers was giving a presentation in Atlanta. During his speech, he described being trapped in the snow and left for dead. Hours into the ordeal, he had a clear vision of his wife and children. Unable to fathom not being with them again, he simply found the energy to stand up. In an amazing display of intuition, he was able to traverse the mountain and find a group of tents, where he was cared for before being taken to safety.

Action is something we must all do to move forward. If we can infuse action with the passion of authentic purpose, the power of our action increases exponentially. Consider the high level of performance you see from athletes at the Olympics when competing for a championship. Think of the humanitarians Martin Luther King, Mother Theresa, and Mahatma Gandhi; their actions were inspired by a greater purpose, something that transcended them. Recall the great heroes Joan of Arc, Winston Churchill, and the millions of unnamed men and women who have performed incredible acts of bravery; all were inspired and acted on a greater purpose. We must find our inspiration, and we must act on it. When we do, the power of our actions will take us much further down the pathway to an extraordinary life.

"Nobody can go back and start a new beginning, but anyone can start today and make a new ending."

-Marianne Williamson

Mindset in A Minute

The Time Is Now

Harness the power of this moment and take purposeful action today

Step 1. Embrace the moment: Understand that it's all you have and, in many ways, the meaning of your life will be determined by how much joy you find in each moment.

Step 2. Understand that everything you do matters: Per the Butterfly Effect, every action you take sends ripples throughout the world that go on forever. Know this, and seek to make all your actions positive and purposeful in your life.

Step 3. Get in the zone: Put yourself in a position to perform at your optimal level. This means getting in a positive mood, quieting your mind, and becoming present in the moment before you take significant action.

Step 4. Be a continuous learner: Understand that in life there is no failure, only feedback. Get comfortable with ambiguity and prepare to adjust as you learn from your experiences.

Step 5. Act on purpose: When you know what you want from your life and what matters, seek to take more and more actions toward your dreams, and eliminate as many non value-added activities from your life as possible.

The Man Who Thinks He Can

If you think you are beaten, you are;
If you think you dare not, you don't.
If you'd like to win, but think you can't
It's almost a cinch that you won't
If you think you'll lose, you're lost,
For out in the world we find
Success begins with a fellow's will;
It's all in the state of mind.

If you think you're outclassed, you are:
You've got to think high to rise.
You've got to be sure of yourself before
You can ever win a prize.
Life's battles don't always go
To the stronger or faster man;
But sooner or later the man who wins
Is the one who thinks he can.

-Walter D. Wintle

Chapter 10

Live Your Dreams

"All our dreams can come true if we have the courage to pursue them."

-Walt Disney

Let the Transformation Begin

Now you've learned the *7 Mindsets,* and it is time to start living them. Personal change can be very difficult. Earlier in the book, we stated that many experts believe over 98% of self-improvement efforts fail. Bryan Tracy, bestselling author and world-renowned life coach, states that the great enemy of personal change is the "Power of Suggestion." No matter how inspired you are to change, you have to execute the change in the same environment and influences that created the very habits you are trying to adjust. Over his long career, Tracy has learned that success is predicated on a sustainability, which requires an empowerment model that becomes part of the Power of Suggestion and delivers information, motivation, and inspiration to help an individual adjust his or her mental habits or mindsets.

We have divided this chapter into two sections. The first contains a list of research-based suggestions and ideas to help you get started and, more importantly, sustain the positive changes you initiate. In section two, we provide an overview of the sustainability process we have tested with several thousand people over the past three years. Personal improvement is a very individual process. In the end, it is up to you and only you to define and execute this change within yourself. We have, however, identified a variety of critical elements that, when implemented, we believe will significantly improve your level of success.

Section One: Suggestions for Sustainability

Radical Self Interest

To increase your chances of success, you have to be able to answer the personal question, "What's in it for me?" The results of your effort must produce something that matters to you. This is where you will get the initial motivation to start the process. Extreme examples of this are when people find out they have a serious medical issue, and they need to make a radical change to their behavior. When this is the case, they become highly motivated to make a change and stick with it. The stakes are high, and there is little room for error. This process is something that you can replicate for other changes you want to make in your life. The best way to light the fire is to envision the new life you desire and the benefits you will reap from your improved effort. Visualizing what your life will look like and how you will feel after you've made the change will help put you in the proper frame of mind.

The Power of the Pack

While the process of change is personal, your chances of success are substantially improved with a collective effort. People who exercise almost always achieve better results when they have a partner or a group of people committed to inspiring and holding each other accountable. A great team is always stronger than the sum of its parts. The point is that any significant life change will require support from others along the way. Many people find a renewed sense of inner strength and resiliency when they help support others going through the same life-changing process as they are. Find a *Mindset*

Buddy, or start your own Ultimate Life Club with friends, coworkers, or family, and experience the power of the pack–when two or more people committed to a common goal do whatever it takes to help each pack member achieve new levels of success.

Measure the Milestones

Most people want instant results and instant gratification when they implement a new approach. Experts agree that to lose weight and sustain it, you should lose approximately one pound a week. This seems too slow for most people, especially when they see an advertisement to lose 10 pounds in 10 days. While it's possible to lose more weight in a short period of time, the term yo-yo dieting exists because it's almost impossible to sustain the weight lost in a rapid process. Know when going into any new routine that true and sustainable change happens slowly. Set small attainable goals that can be measured on a daily or weekly basis. It really is the little things that, when done over and over again, create the greatest long-term results. It's critical to recognize even the most marginal of milestones. This reinforces your resolve and builds confidence that you are getting where you want to go. Change comes through the execution of different action; new and purposeful action that takes you places and creates new growth that did not exist before.

Expect the Unexpected

Everyone encounters roadblocks when they attempt to make changes in their lives. Sometimes, we can anticipate what those roadblocks might be, and other times we get completely surprised. There is a major difference between how people react to the challenging roadblocks that almost always show up. Typically, the people who push through the roadblocks and make the positive changes are the ones who expected to hit a roadblock in the first place. They didn't necessarily know what it would be, but they knew it would be something. They mentally prepared ahead of time, so that when obstacles got in their way, they would find ways around them. Whatever the obstacles turned out to be, the people would persevere and push forward. The groups that typically fail to sustain their change have an entirely different reaction to setbacks and roadblocks. When something gets in their way and temporarily halts their progress, they view these things as proof that they can't make the changes needed or that they knew it was going to be too hard. The obstacles become less of an excuse and more of a validation that the process for change is flawed. Our advice to you is to expect the unexpected and prepare to make changes, no matter what it takes, and whenever needed. As Willie Jolley states in his book, *It Only Takes a Minute to Change Your Life*, "A setback ain't nothin' but a setup for a comeback."

Section Two: The 7 Mindsets Experience

Over the past few years, we have taught the *7 Mindsets* to thousands of people, primarily teenagers and educators. We understood that real change gets measured over time, and that most people would forget what they learned unless we helped them retain the content. Life is one of the best teachers, and our students needed to experience situations over time that challenged what they learned.

We developed and gradually improved a process and set of tools to help them deepen their understanding of the mindsets, as well as activate and sustain them in their life. We wanted to be there for them, and also wanted to develop a process that could scale in order to reach and support millions globally. Internally, we call this Mindset Maintenance, a year-round process that engages and supports individuals when, where, and how they need it most. Listed below are the major components:

1. Daily Quotes

Every day, we distribute a quote connected to one of the *7 Mindsets*. Feedback indicates that the quotes help people focus on an important mindset, and reminds them of what they learned.

2. Weekly Story

Every Wednesday, we distribute a short, inspiring story detailing how one of the mindsets has been used in someone's life. Stories include little known facts about famous people, the ultra-successful, as well as unique personal experiences from the 7 Mindsets Team. Each letter includes a brief call to action connecting the message with a method you can implement immediately.

Both are available when you like our page at www.Facebook.com/7Mindsets.

3. Live to Give Challenge

Every July, we sponsor the *Live to Give* challenge to help students live the mindsets and make an impact in their community. The *Live to Give* Challenge is a program that encourages students to connect their passion with a social cause they believe in to benefit others in their community or around the world. Students have 37 days to initiate and complete a project. They upload a five-minute video describing their project and the impact they made. The videos are made available for the general public to watch and vote for their favorite *Live to Give* project. These projects take place all over the world, and the feedback we've received is amazing. The students deepen their understanding of the mindsets while putting them to good use. Projects inspire other students, as well as strangers, to embrace the mindsets.

4. Online Learning Experience and Life Plan Development

The 7 Mindset MasterClass Online Experience provides video lessons on all of the 7 Mindsets and the tools needed to create your own Life Plan, so you can undertake the process of realizing your dreams. Check it out at www.7MindsetsMasterClass.com

5. Stay in Touch

Join our mailing list to be notified of new developments and resources by emailing us at info@7Mindsets.com.

Learning the 7 Mindsets Is Eye-Opening
Living Them Is Life-Changing

This book was written to provide you with an understanding of the *7 Mindsets* and a blueprint to activate them in your life. Over the years, we've learned that sustaining this information requires ongoing effort. We encourage you to follow the advice and suggestions we've included, and are confident they will help you activate and sustain what you've learned.

"You cannot hold a torch to light another's path without brightening your own."

-Rumi

Chapter 11

Empowering Youth

"A teacher is measured not by the number of students they teach but rather the masters they create."

-Indian Proverb

Our Magic Wand

In the beginning of the book, we warned you that we have a hidden agenda. We believe that many of the world's challenges are only going to be solved through the hearts and minds of young people. Our mission is to empower youth to live their Ultimate Lives and bring positive change to their communities. We believe we can help create a generational shift in which young people live to their greatest potential and seek exciting, creative, and meaningful ways to make a positive impact on the world.

The final phase of our research focused on the most effective ways to empower youth to live the *7 Mindsets*. Over the past quarter century, we have helped start some of the world's leading youth empowerment organizations. We have created an educational software company with the sole purpose of utilizing technology to maximize student potential. Through all of this, we have developed a revolutionary process for empowering youth.

Not all young people are the same. The empowerment light bulb comes on at different times and through different channels for each student. Once it's on, the new energy must be sustained, since statistics show that without a sustainable solution, the vast majority of youth will fall back into their old behavior patterns within just two weeks. For this reason, we have developed a teaching model that reaches the maximum number of youth and sustains the process for the time required to facilitate positive personal change in a lasting way.

The 10 Ultimate Youth Empowerment Techniques

1. Inspire Inward Thinking

In his book, *The New Earth*, Eckhart Tolle does a masterful job of describing the human ego, how it has evolved, and its very destructive nature in our individual and collective paths toward a better life and world. We associate ourselves with, and compute our worth on, things that are external and always temporary. This extrinsic process, Tolle says, will always lead to suffering. Ultimately, the first and most critical step toward self-improvement is to break through this ego-driven motivation and find motivation intrinsically. In other words, become your authentic self.

Eliminating ego is easier said than done. Since the ultimate aim of ego elimination is enlightenment, the process is one we must spend our entire lives developing. The most important thing is to start that process as soon as possible, preferably before bad habits and excessive baggage build up. The sooner a young person starts this process, the better off he or she will be.

Our approach to youth empowerment is centered on the concept, "from the inside out." In every step of our process, we first ask students to look inside for answers before looking outward for solutions. We demonstrate our quirkiness and seek to build great pride in our students' uniqueness. Lastly, we continually modify our language to promote this. For example, rather than telling a student we are proud of them, we suggest that they should be proud of themselves. While this is very subtle, it is critical because it begins teaching them to look inside for validation, a critical step toward becoming intrinsically motivated.

2. Expand Time Preference

In the early 1990's, much of our work was based on a study done on a concept called *Time Preference*. Today, there is research being done on a concept known as *Possible Selves Theory*. Both bodies of work look at the impact of a student's perception of the future. The studies show that the average teenager has a *time preference* of roughly 12 to 24 hours when making a decision. Essentially, that means that they are assessing the implications of the decision based on what the consequences or benefits are over the next 12 to 24 hours. So, for example, when taking drugs or drinking alcohol, they are assessing whether or not they will get caught. When dropping out of school, they may be considering the fact that they do not have to do homework or deal with a teacher or an adverse situation in school. When deciding whether or not to read a book, they are asking what they are going to get out of it in the next 24 hours. You can imagine how this mentality can foster some very destructive decisions.

In the 1990s, when we taught entrepreneurship to inner city youth, the focus was to give the youth a new and more positive perspective of their future. Many had trouble picturing themselves finishing high school, let alone going to college. Very few imagined lives filled with happiness and joy. Their short time preference often led to some very negative, life-altering choices. Through teaching entrepreneurship, we were able to provide many with a new and more positive view of the future and a clear path to achieving a new dream. Not every student is interested in starting their own business, so today we've learned to get the same positive results by teaching students the *7 Mindsets to Live Your Ultimate Life*. The same underlying factor holds true: students begin to expect more from their lives.

What happens when a young person begins to value their future is exciting. It starts to impact their daily decision-making process. They now see how dropping out of school, taking drugs, or committing a crime can damage their dreams. Those dreams become precious, and the students are not willing to jeopardize them. There was a study in the 1990s which showed that if a young person's time preference is expanded by even a few days or weeks, they are 90% less likely to make catastrophic, life-changing decisions like doing drugs, getting pregnant, or dropping out of school.

A vital step in our teaching methodology is the infusion of constant forward thinking in everything we do. The intent is to create in each of our students a positive and far-reaching view of their future. We do this through our Ultimate Life planning process. We encourage students to envision their Ultimate Life, and then begin a process of helping them plan it. Our primary goal is to expand their time preference while creating a positive mental image of their future.

3. Leverage Radical Self-Interest

One of the greatest challenges of today's education process is the perception of irrelevance students have toward the curriculum they are being taught. When we ask our students why English matters or why math is relevant, we often get surface answers at best. The most common answer is that they just need to pass the class to graduate high school. When we probe further, it becomes apparent that very few students have made a connection between what they are learning in school and how it will benefit or positively affect them in their lives.

As we introduce concepts, the very first thing we do is make a connection to what we call their "radical self-interest." Students must want to learn the information or they will not fully engage in the learning process. What makes them want to learn something? It could be a very clear connection between the subject and how it will benefit them. For example, just about every teenager would like to grow up to be a millionaire, or achieve a high level of financial freedom. When they learn that only 3% of adults retire as millionaires, they wonder why. This creates an opportunity to teach them financial literacy and other important skills. We're using money as one example, but the same is true about happiness, finding a job about which they are passionate, and solving problems in the world. If you can make the connection to what they care about, you can then teach them what they want and what they need to know. Once this connection is made, a teacher can begin facilitating the learning process.

4.   Create a Multi-Sensory Experience

Thousands of books have been written on the best way to teach children. We all have our own presentation style, typically based on that with which we are comfortable. There are tests such as DISC and Myers Briggs, which attempt to define who we are and how we best work. Ultimately, what it boils down to is that we all absorb and process information differently. An effective teaching program should leverage whatever tools are at our disposal to impact every student and learning style in the classroom.

We use a multitude of approaches: we leverage visual imagery and photographs to create indelible and memorable images; we infuse video throughout our programs, typically emotionally-anchored video to drive home the lessons; at critical times, we play music to create emotional responses and use the lyrics to make a deeper connection with our students. Technology and related tools can invigorate learning exponentially. Additionally, we execute activities that play to kinesthetic learners and facilitate real-world programs that engage our students in the critical actions required to truly embed the new concepts. Students participate in introspective processes and are continually asked to participate. The overriding strategy is to deliver a consistent and powerful message through multiple mediums that allows all students to grasp and ultimately apply the concepts.

5.   Utilize Storytelling to Anchor Message

Mark Twain is considered one of the greatest orators of all time. There are legends of him showing up at an event and unexpectedly being asked to give a presentation on something about which he had no prior notice or ability to prepare. In minutes, he could prepare and deliver a phenomenal presentation inspiring everyone in the audience. People from around the world were amazed at his ability to inspire. Fascinated, they would seek to understand what he did. Twain, knowing that his talent was unique, was unwilling to share his secret. It wasn't until late in his life that he finally shared his approach.

Twain's storytelling was much more a science than an art. He had hundreds of stories that he used in his presentations. However, he didn't just tell the stories, he perfected them. He would spend hours upon hours refining each. He would decide specifically where he would pause and which syllable in each word he would emphasize.

Perhaps more importantly, Twain could use any one of his stories to anchor multiple messages. He might tell a story about his childhood to demonstrate mistakes he had made or challenges he had overcome. He might tell the same story to build a relationship with his audience or share a secret he had learned about life. The genius of this resulted in some of the greatest presentations of his day. Given a few minutes and a topic, he could quickly pull his stories together and align them with the key message and flow of his presentation. The end result was an engaging and powerful presentation that inspired and entertained.

Our approach to youth empowerment leverages this storytelling model. It is said that a young person today can focus between three and five minutes on any given topic. Our entire instructional process is designed around a series of three to five minute vignettes. We use stories to anchor our key lessons.

6. Facilitate Teambuilding

Perhaps the most powerful thing we can do as educators is create an environment in which our students support each other and begin to coach and mentor one another. When we create an environment where students can share openly and feel supported, the empowerment process is supercharged. Once the imaginary walls are broken down, you can get to the heart of the matter, and students can act from a place unobstructed by fear and doubt. This is absolutely essential to creating an effective learning environment.

One of our board members is Scott Rigsby. Scott is the first double amputee (both legs) to complete the grueling Iron Man competition held in Hawaii each year. In his book, *Unthinkable*, he describes his initial attempts as lone individual efforts that ultimately came up short. Rigsby says, "If you can accomplish your dream alone, you are not dreaming big enough." When he began to embrace the help and support of others, he made himself vulnerable; he ultimately opened up the channels that provided the much-needed support he required to fulfill his dream.

Too often, the vast majority of us are afraid to ask for help when everyone around us would love nothing more than to help. In Jack Canfield's book, *The Aladdin Factor*, he describes the common mentality of people who feel too insecure to ask for help. To them, it is a weakness to need counseling for their marriage, assistance with a task, or money for their business or idea. It is the folks that have the courage to ask for help who receive the critical support required to achieve success.

We must create an environment where students are aware of this critical success factor, and which promotes and rewards the simple action of being vulnerable and asking for a little help. In our live events, we focus on building a spirit of cooperation and support among our students. The first step in the process is demonstrating our own vulnerability and making the initial connection as a flawed human being. The second step is to execute a series of activities that connect people and build critical trust. Finally, throughout all our programs, we give our students the opportunity to share, encouraging openness and the seeking of guidance and support.

7. Embrace Creativity

Ask most people if they are creative and their knee-jerk response is usually "no." That's a shame for a number of reasons. It's a shame because most of us have a very skewed and limited definition of creativity. It's also a shame because, once upon a time, creativity was part of who we were, almost like another limb. So what happened? How did we lose our creativity? For most of us, it happened early in life, and more than likely when we started school. Before we entered a regimented environment where our thinking was roped like a calf at a rodeo, our minds were filled with amazing and wonderful thoughts. There was nothing we couldn't do, no place we couldn't visit, no adventure out of reach. That's because imagination fueled our creativity.

Creativity is not limited to the arts, although the arts are populated by those who never lost their gifts of imagination. Creativity is found in the way we think, the way we problem-solve, the way we act and interact with people, and the way we envision the lives we are meant to live.

Because we embrace creativity and understand the power of imagination, our programs are infused with both. We encourage young people to reconnect with their creative genius, and we help them fire up their imaginations. Instead of believing there are only a limited number of ways to do things, we teach young people that the sky is the limit. We also teach them to "expect the unexpected," because the creative process is often not the shortest distance between two points. Sometimes imagination leads us on an amazing journey to areas of thinking we never expected—usually with some amazingly unexpected results.

8. Promote Constant Growth

Albert Einstein is among the greatest geniuses that ever lived. While he was a very capable math student, his math skills fell far short of many of the scientists of his day. He would often say, "If I could just get a better handle on the math, I could do so much more." He worked very hard his entire life developing his math skills. As a matter of fact, when he died, there was a tablet of paper next to his bed on which he was scribbling math equations. Until the day he died, he constantly sought the opportunity to improve himself. In John Maxwell's bestselling book, *The 21 Irrefutable Laws of Leadership*, he calls this constant yearning for growth the "Law of Process." He tells that Teddy Roosevelt was studying new military concepts up until he died, and that after his death, a book on the subject was found under his pillow.

One significant research effort on this topic was performed by Carol Dweck for her book, *Mindset*. In that book, she states the critical difference between people who achieve success and those who don't is what she calls the "Growth" mindset. She describes two types of mindsets. The first is of a young person who believes they are either talented or not, and that life is a measurement and a validation of this talent. These people struggle in life, and are unable to deal with or overcome life's natural challenges and adversities. The second "mindset" is based on growth, and describes a young person constantly seeking to learn and grow, undaunted by failure, and constantly aspiring to new and rewarding challenges. These people achieve much higher success. Her body of evidence and the logic behind her arguments are almost impossible to dispute, and we certainly agree wholeheartedly.

Effective education is not about teaching concepts, but rather facilitating the process of learning. Our approach to youth empowerment embodies this perspective. We singularly focus on the process, not the answers or responses of our students. We continually drive them to take action, and understand that it is the learning and adjustment that are important, not necessarily the direct result on the action. We communicate the importance of being a continual learner, and of gaining knowledge and wisdom from all experiences, including the perceived negative or adverse circumstances of one's life. Fred DeLuca, founder of SUBWAY®, may have summed this up best when we interviewed him. His philosophy is to start small and finish big. The expansion of SUBWAY into the world's largest restaurant franchise, as with all big accomplishments, did not happen in one sweeping moment of inspired action; it was a series of thousands upon thousands of smaller but equally inspired steps, all of which drove to, and ultimately culminated in, a single significant and measurable accomplishment.

9. Foster Big Dreams

Each time we speak at a school, it is almost instantaneously apparent how effective the school or organization is at educating their students. It boils down to one word: expectations. Not just expectations of the students themselves, but those of their friends, of the world around them, and perhaps most importantly, their futures. In their book, *Do Hard Things*, teenage brothers Alex and Brett Harris express frustration at a world in which adults expect very little from teenagers. The two of them have had extraordinary success and accomplishment in their young lives. They attribute it to the fact that their parents and mentors expected more from them, and therefore they expected more from themselves, ultimately driving them to much higher levels of achievement.

Michelangelo once said, "The greatest tragedy is not in setting your goals too high and falling short, it is in setting your sights too low and hitting your mark." Our lives must be about maximizing our potential to positively impact the world and create the greatest level of joy and meaning possible. What Michelangelo was saying is that most of us are leaving massive amounts of joy and fulfillment on the table. We need to be cautious because we are inadvertently stealing the idealism away from our youth. It is idealism and a belief in the future that will facilitate the change this world so desperately needs.

It is essential that we not only give our children back their dreams, but also foster and help nurture those dreams.

At the core of all our programs is a positive envisioning of the future. We are constantly working to recalibrate our students' expectations by continually driving them to expect more out of their lives. We bring this way of thinking into all areas of their lives including relationships, health, finances, and careers. As we stated earlier, people of great achievement have come to know that the only limitation in their lives is the size of their dreams, and perhaps the time they have to achieve them.

10. Celebrate Ambiguity

One of our business partners, Mitchell Schlimer, hosted a national radio show called *Let's Talk Business* for eight years, on which he interviewed successful men, women, and authors who have written about successful people. These interviews comprise a great number of the accounts referenced in this book. Mitch often describes one attribute that separates great entrepreneurs from everyone else as what he calls "comfort with ambiguity." Most of us find comfort in predictability. We want to come across problems we have answers for and situations we have been in before. What we do not like is the unknown. When we do not have answers and the outcomes are unknown, fear takes over and paralyzes us from taking the very steps that are critical to overcoming the challenges.

Men and women of great achievement learn to embrace ambiguity. In *The 7 Spiritual Laws of Success*, Deepak Chopra identified the same concept as "The Wisdom of Uncertainty." According to Chopra, it is the unknown that spawns the creative process required to develop new and innovative solutions, and then grow and expand as an individual. In a world where all is known, Chopra says that the best tomorrow can be is a stale copy of today, and what fun could there ever be in that? In his mind, this mentality is not only a crucial ingredient for success, but one that must be well-developed in order to be truly happy in a dynamic and ever-changing world where ambiguity and uncertainty are no longer the exception, but the rule.

Early in our programs, we work with students on their dreams. We tell them to focus on the *what* and *why*, and not worry about the *how*. If the steps to their dreams are obvious, they are clearly not very big dreams. We tell them rather than focusing on the *how*, just trust their genius and embrace the creative process of solving problems or overcoming obstacles on the path to their goals and dreams. Another critical component of the creative process is risk taking. Our youth must be excited, not just comfortable, about taking risks to pursue their passions. Our programs are a place where risk and failure are not only tolerated, but celebrated. This is all an effort to get them comfortable with ambiguity, or at least to look at it much differently than they ever have before.

Conclusion

There are many ways to educate and empower youth. The 10 techniques listed have proven to be highly effective for teens from diverse backgrounds and many parts of the world. We believe any one of these can significantly improve the learning environment, and that incorporating all of them can radically redefine how students are taught. Combined with the content of the *7 Mindsets*, we have discovered a magic wand with the potential to revolutionize education and empower millions of students to live their Ultimate Lives and make a meaningful impact on the world.

"The teacher who is indeed wise does not bid you to enter the house of his wisdom but rather leads you to the threshold of your mind."

-Kahlil Gibran

Afterword

The world faces many great challenges, from increasing violence to global warming to persistent poverty, and it is often difficult to see realistic solutions. In addition to massive global issues, our communities and families are facing their own complex challenges. As Einstein said, "We can't solve problems by using the same kind of thinking we used when we created them." We believe the *7 Mindsets* are the new way of thinking needed today. Positive change is possible, and it will come from an often-overlooked place: the hearts and minds of our youth, one student at a time.

Our goal is nothing short of a global mind-shift, essentially a quantum leap in the way we think about ourselves, our world, and those who inhabit it with us. We often think of quantum leaps as massively complex events. The reality is that the great shifts in our world were the result of narrowly focused efforts. Imagine if all children learn the *7 Mindsets* as seamlessly as they learn the ABCs.

We think this can be accomplished in seven hours and sustained in seven minutes a day. Through our process, students will move from learning the *7 Mindsets* to living them. We can teach parents, educators, and youth leaders to facilitate this learning, and through technology, we can empower and support youth globally.

Imagine a world in which young people identify their unique gifts and share them with the world to their greatest ability. They will dream bigger, live passionately, empower others, embrace accountability, appreciate life, give unconditionally, and act with purpose. We imagine this every day, and we've created a youth empowerment movement to bring it to fruition.

If you believe in our mission, join us!

- Live the *7 Mindsets* and be the best you possible!
- Share this book or recommend it to others. For every book purchased, we will donate one to a deserving student through the Magic Wand Foundation.
- Send feedback on the book to info@7Mindsets.com.
- Develop your own life plan to reach your dreams through the 7 Mindsets MasterClass Online Experience. www.7MindsetsMasterClass.com
- Bring us to your community to keynote a conference, deliver a seminar to employees or students, sign our books, or collaborate on a youth empowerment project. Learn more at www.7Mindsets.com
- Stay connected by email at info@7Mindsets.com or receive a daily morning mindset and a weekly Mindset in Practice story every Wednesday if you like us on Facebook at www.Facebook.com/7Mindsets.

When you live the 7 Mindsets, you no longer need to find a magic wand; you will become the wand, and realize you've had the power all along.

Live Your Dreams,

Scott & Jeff

Bring the Mindsets to Your Classroom, School, Organization, Company or Community

"We make a living by what we get, but we make a life by what we give."
-Winston Churchill

We have developed a number of programs to help bring the *7 Mindsets* to your community, including teacher training workshops, student seminars, multi-day programs, summer camps, and customized events. Additionally, we have developed curriculum and online learning tools available for educators, youth leaders, parents, and socially-minded individuals and companies. Please review the list below and contact us to discuss how we might assist you with your youth empowerment plans.

College and Career Readiness Compliance Made Easy!

Empowering students and helping prepare them for their best lives is a wonderful privilege. By shifting (just a little) how they view the world around them and their place in it, we can see positive transformation occur that is immediate and permanent. Improved graduation rates, higher test scores, engaged students of character, and decreased behavior issues are all outcomes of a new mindset.

This is a Life Changing Revolution. This is 7 Mindsets.

7 Mindsets Academy is a proven character education and youth empowerment program that is changing the way students think, interact and live. It started with a question: What drives long-term happiness and success among people, regardless of age, ethnicity or background? That research identified 7 mental habits foundational to an enriched life. Based on simple, powerful language to teach and activate success strategies, the 7 Mindsets program empowers students to avoid risk behaviors, pursue their dreams and make a positive difference in the world.

This isn't about gaining more knowledge or learning a new skill. 7 Mindsets is a proactive, fundamental shift in the character development of a person. Designed to implement school-wide or by individual classroom over one semester for just 30-60 minutes a week, 7 Mindsets Academy will increase academic performance, motivation, and resilience among your students.

www.7MindsetsAcademy.com

7 Mindsets MasterClass is an online learning experience teaching the actions and attitudes that lead to happiness and success through inspirational storytelling, a Life Plan, and the Mindset Maintenance program. Learn to build meaningful relationships, connect with others, embrace the moment, act with purpose, and ultimately lead your best life.

www.7MindsetsMasterclass.com

7 Mindsets University is a certification program delivered by the foremost personal empowerment experts in the world. Master proven strategies that empower others to dream bigger, tap into their passions, work better with others, be more accountable, and act with a greater sense of purpose. Learn how to deliver the 7 Mindsets program to invigorate your classroom, community center, practice, or business.

www.7MindsetsUniversity.com

7 Mindset Partners

Want to expand your existing business? 7 Mindsets is a proven character education program changing the way young people and adults think, interact and live. It is based on years of extensive research that uncovered how the world's happiest and most successful people think and act. By becoming a trained and certified Mindset Coach, you are equipped to launch or build upon a thriving practice around the 7 Mindset revolution.

Life changing seminars and workshops from renowned 7 Mindsets speakers are available around the globe. The audience will be energized and invigorated with a new blueprint for happiness, meaning and success by inspiring stories, powerful videos, and engaging activities.

www.7MindsetsSpeakers.com

7 Mindsets@Work is focused on motivating and energizing your employees to maximize their potential and the execution of your company's mission and vision. Executed by dynamic speakers, our

team teaches your employees the 7 Mindsets and aligns them to your critical business objectives:

Everything is Possible@ Work–Create a culture of higher employee expectations and individual contribution to company success.

Passion First@Work – Increase productivity, employee morale, job satisfaction, and overall retention.

We Are Connected@Work – Facilitate greater cooperation among employees and enhanced teamwork.

100% Accountable@Work – Build an environment of ownership, where employees seek constant growth and greater impact on organizational success.

Attitude of Gratitude@Work – Build a positive, optimistic culture where employees are happier and supportive of one another.

Live to Give@Work – Anchor your organization around a common purpose and inspire employees to new levels of achievement.

The Time is Now@Work – Energize your organization with a culture of action and a healthy sense of urgency around company goals.

www.7MindsetsAtWork.com

The Ultimate Life Summit (ULS) is a one-of-a-kind, action-packed, life-changing experience held each year! The ULS is a cutting edge, multi-cultural adventure that focuses on team dynamics, life planning, and leadership qualities. This empowering adventure is anchored by the 7 Mindsets™ essential to living an Ultimate Life – one filled with passion, happiness, and extraordinary success.

www.UltimateLifeSummit.com

7 Mindsets Entrepreneurship Camp is a unique gathering of students from local communities. From three to five days, motivated teens convene for a life-changing experience. Attendees learn entrepreneurship fundamentals, as well as the mindsets and skillsets to live their Ultimate Life – one filled with passion, happiness, and extraordinary success!

www.7mindsetsEntrepreneurship.com

About the Authors

Scott Shickler is one of the world's leading experts on youth empowerment. The *Wall Street Journal* referred to him as a serial and parallel entrepreneur due to the number of businesses he started in diverse industries. Collectively, his companies have grossed over $37 million, with businesses ranging from software to seminars and real estate to restaurants. Shickler is the author or co-author of 8 books, including *The 7 Mindsets to Live Your Ultimate Life* and *The Ultimate Entrepreneur*. Scott also wrote the Boy Scout Merit Badge booklet on entrepreneurship. He has been featured in a variety of media including CNN, ABC & NBC News, *The New York Times and The Wall Street Journal*. Shickler is currently the CEO and founder of Excent Corporation, a multi-million dollar education company serving millions of students and educators throughout the world. Scott is the co-creator of The 7 Mindsets and a dynamic speaker who has addressed over 100,000 people on the mindsets of living their Ultimate Life and making a positive impact on the world. He grew up in New York and now lives in Atlanta with his wife and two sons. Scott is a graduate of Fordham University and the co-founder of the Magic Wand Foundation, a non-profit organization devoted to empowering youth to live their dreams.

About the Authors

Jeff Waller is a leading visionary on personal achievement and youth empowerment. He is the cofounder of Excent Corporation, a multi-million dollar education company serving millions of students and educators throughout the world. Jeff is the co-creator of The 7 Mindsets, an organization focused on the delivery of cutting edge empowerment models distributed through scalable technologies and on sustainable platforms. His work includes the development of the revolutionary *7 Mindsets* program and the *Ultimate Life Summit*, a blended empowerment program that uses dynamic live seminars along with existing and emerging tools to sustain youth empowerment initiatives. A motivational speaker, Jeff is also the co-founder of the Magic Wand Foundation, an organization dedicated to empowering youth to live their dreams and make a positive impact on the world. He has dedicated the last decade to learning and understanding the critical elements that define high achievers. Jeff has worked with over 5,000 teens to help them identify their passions in life and encouraging them to pursue their dreams. Prior to his work with teens, Jeff was a highly successful business strategist, working with large Fortune 500 companies to develop technology strategies. Jeff lives in Atlanta with his wife and three children. He holds a degree from The Georgia Institute of Technology.

Resources

Our team is involved in many organizations and events focused on empowering youth globally. It is the integrated mission at the core of everything we do. Here are several with which we are heavily involved:

Excent Corporation, and the 7 Mindsets

Excent® provides data solutions and direct training services to empower students and educators in both special and general education. School district success and students reaching their potential is our passion. At **Excent**, we believe the path to success begins with empowerment, and that access to the right resources can make all the difference in reaching true potential and achieving big dreams.

7 Mindsets™ is a business unit within Excent that delivers programs centered on the 7 Mindsets, which are based on years of extensive research on personal achievement and more than 100 combined years working directly with over 200,000 youth. Through our experience, we have learned that every young person possesses incredible potential. Our methodology allows them to uncover this potential, take pride in their uniqueness, and begin putting their skills and interests to work building better futures for themselves and the world around them. www.Excent.com

Magic Wand Foundation

The **Magic Wand Foundation** is a non-profit organization that empowers young people to find happiness, live their dreams, and develop a passion for making a positive impact on the world. Their goal is to empower teens to take purposeful action in the present so they can create a life of greater joy and meaning. The Magic Wand Foundation provides scholarships to mindset training programs to facilitate this vision. www.MagicWandFoundation.org

Acknowledgements

"If you can accomplish your dream alone, you are not dreaming big enough."

-*Scott Rigsby*

This book is the culmination of our life's work, lives blessed with many extraordinary individuals along the way. We can only accomplish so much as individuals and, until we learn to work with, for, and through others, our big dreams will never be fulfilled. Along our journey, many individuals have taught us, coached us, and inspired us to be better and do better. All our dreams will forever be shared with those who have supported and inspired us along the way. It's virtually impossible to thank every person who has played a role in the research and writing of this book, but we do want to highlight some very special people:

Mitch Schlimer (Doc) – Mitch's experience and research has driven much of our thinking and methodology. More importantly, his friendship and guidance have brought us through many challenges and given us the strength and courage to pursue our destiny.

Juan Casimiro (Papi) – Juan has dedicated his life to helping youth. He is an inspiration to all who know him and understand the depths of his empathy and love for the next generation. He is the "real deal" and a blessing, not just to us, but to all who have ever come in contact with him.

Nashid Sharrief – Once a high school math teacher in Detroit, Nashid has shown us what is required to truly empower teens. Through his guidance, we now understand that the only way to achieve our mission is to not only empower teens but also empower the parents and educators that support them.

Vince Coyner – All great products require a collective effort. An essential element is critical thinking, Vince has made us look at our conclusions differently. He has challenged the very assumptions of our work, and has driven our collective thinking forward immensely.

Wes Williams – Wes is an example of what we want for all youth. A young successful businessman, he has given valuable time, energy, and resources to us unconditionally. There is no doubt the great successes in his life are a direct function of his powerful giving spirit.

Tim O'Rourke – Tim was one of the first to believe in our mission and commit himself to our cause. The support of a man such as Tim has given us great confidence in our work and motivated us to sustain our effort through many trying times.

David Bakelman – David is a seasoned social entrepreneur and as giving a person as we know. Through his experience, network, and amazing talent, we were able to launch our mission. Through his constant guidance, we have been able to succeed in creating a wonderful platform for success.

Lara Hodgson – An extraordinary woman, she is the great connector. Through her, we have met people we could only dream of meeting, we have created extraordinary relationships, and we have learned to create our dreams with and through others and their organizations.

Bernardo Flores – Perhaps the kindest young soul we have ever met. Bernardo provided us critical input from a teenager's perspective. He also has inspired us in many ways and given us great confidence in our future, a future in the hands of extraordinary young men and women such as him.

Lourdes Mola – Lourdes allowed us to run our first Ultimate Life Program at Disney World. Through her, we were able to have extraordinary success and have built our flagship event, The Ultimate Life Summit, into an incredible catalyst to our mission of empowering youth globally.

George Moore – Among the most extraordinary young people we have ever met, he has inspired us to take our message to Europe. Each day he drives us to do better, to reach more youth, and maximize the positive impact we are having.

Stephanie Johnston – An incredible young woman from Minnesota, Stephanie has taught us how to bring our methodology into a community and work with all interested parties in creating a sustainable positive impact at a local level.

Chris Koke – The creative spirit of our organization, Chris continually drives us to think differently, and is consistently defining many of the greatest aspects of our work. He is a man who has learned how to enjoy the moment and teaches us this lesson each and every day.

Adam Stern – A true hero to us, Adam has been with us since day one. He has persevered through many frustrations and stood by us through and through. He has been instrumental in so many aspects of our success, and we thank him for the gift of his time and positive energy.

Leslie Williams – Among our first supporters, she committed to our mission enthusiastically. She has brought us such joy and warm-heartedness. Since day one, she has embodied our mission and commitment to young people.

Ruth Baez – A wonderfully loving woman, she has helped build our mission in the Dominican Republic and Latin America. Only through her could we have gotten mothers to believe in who we are. Never without a smile, she embodies everything we want to be.

Jorge Olmos – Jorge is our great blessing in Mexico. Passionate about teaching and empowering youth, he has helped us take the *7 Mindsets* to his country. Today, Mexico is one of our largest areas served outside of the United States, largely due to the wonderful work that Jorge is doing.

Jorge Posada – One of our great heroes, Jorge is truly one of the Ultra-Successful. In a life measured by joy in each moment, he is perhaps the most successful person we know. It is a gift to know him and a blessing to be part of his life.

Donna Walker – A special person and a special life focused on empowering youth. She has inspired us in so many ways and has been a major part of our mission since its inception.

Duane Moyer – We have been working with Duane for over 20 years. Our paths parted for a short while but we are back together. It has been such a wonderful journey with Duane and may our paths never part again. His guidance and project management have made all the difference.

David Craig – David joined our team in 2009 after supporting our work for years. Now one of our greatest assets, he has helped us create sustainability to our mission, developing a business that will empower youth for many years to come. David is a great friend and we look forward to our continued journey together.

Alice Ormiston – Alice is often the unsung hero. She is involved closely in everything we do. She has been instrumental in all our success and in every aspect of our business and foundation. She is a trusted advisor and provides the essential support that allows us to function at our best.

Rand Cabus – Rand is the creative and artistic genius that gives life to many of our ideas, including book cover designs, logos, websites, and countless items designed to empower and inspire youth to live their dreams.

April Farlow – April is one of our great teachers. She has taught us how to be better, and challenged us to get more from ourselves than we ever realized possible. We look forward to helping each other live our dreams together.

Vinnie Begley – Vinnie is a wonderful partner. An incredible writer and creative genius, he has been instrumental in helping us develop much of the content and curriculum that allows us to truly make a difference in the lives of youth.

Ultimate Life Summit Students – All our early development efforts centered on the Ultimate Life Summit we conduct each year at Disney World in Florida. We would like to thank each and every one of the students who have attended. You are the reason we do what we do. The future is bright because it is in now in your hands.

The Excent Team – All our efforts are made possible by the incredible team we have at Excent Corp. Your commitment to youth empowerment and the education system is inspirational. You are the foundation of everything the 7 Mindsets is doing. A special thanks to our customers who we serve gladly and who empower us to empower youth.

The Magic Wand Foundation Board – It is so wonderful having such a caring and influential team supporting us. Your commitment to our foundation is humbling, and we thank you for all you do from the bottom of our hearts.

Appendix A:
People Interviewed and Studied

We researched and interviewed more than 400 individuals. Due to limited space we are listing about 100 here. The complete list can be found at www.7Mindsets.com.

John Adams, Founding Father of the United States
*Mark Albion, Author: Making A Life, Making A Living
*Wally Amos, Founder: Famous Amos Cookies
Maya Angelou, Author and Poet
Aristotle, Greek Philosopher
Arthur Ashe, Champion Tennis Player
Mary Kay Ashe, Founder: Mary Kay Cosmetics
Marcus Aurelius, Roman Emperor and Philosopher
*Sir Richard Branson, Billionaire, Founder: The Virgin Group
*Les Brown, Motivational Speaker & Author: Live Your Dreams
*Marcus Buckingham, Author: Now Discover Your Strengths
Warren Buffet, Billionaire Investor and Author
*Jack Canfield, Co-Author: Chicken Soup for the Soul
Andrew Carnegie, American Industrialist and Businessman
Dr. Ben Carson, Neurosurgeon
Deepak Chopra, Author
Winston Churchill, British Prime Minister During WWII
*Ben Cohen & Jerry Greenfield, Founders: Ben & Jerry's Ice Cream
*Jim Collins, Author: Good to Great
Confucius, Ancient Chinese Social Philosopher
Steven Covey, Author: The 7 Habits of Highly Effective People
Leonardo da Vinci, Renaissance Artist, Architect, Scientist, and Engineer
Henry David Thoreau, Famous American Author and Philosopher

*Fred DeLuca, Founder: SUBWAY®
Walt Disney, Founder: Walt Disney Company
*Wayne Dyer, Author
Amelia Earhart, First Woman to Fly Across the Atlantic
Thomas Edison, Industrialist and Inventor
Albert Einstein, Scientist
Ralph Waldo Emerson, Author and Philosopher
Debbie Fields, Founder: Mrs. Fields Cookies
Anne Frank, Author and Victim of Holocaust
Viktor Frankl, Psychologist, Author, and Holocaust Survivor
Benjamin Franklin, American Founding Father, Inventor, and Author
Mahatma Gandhi, Political and Ideological Leader
Bill Gates, Co-Founder: Microsoft
*Michael Gerber, Author: The E-Myth
Khalil Gibran, Artist, Author and Poet
Jane Goodall, Internationally Acclaimed Primate Researcher
Alexander Graham Bell, Inventor of Telephone
*Earl Graves, Founder: Black Enterprise Magazine
Bethany Hamilton, Teenage Surfer Who Lost Arm in Shark Attack
*Mark Victor Hansen, Co-Author: Chicken Soup for the Soul
Carlos Slim Helu, Wealthiest Man in the World, Mexico
Napoleon Hill, Author: Think and Grow Rich
Patrick Henry Hughes, Inspirational Musician
Paul Hewson (Bono), Singer, U2, Humanitarian
Wayne Huizenga, Entrepreneur, Owner: Miami Dolphins
Thomas Jefferson, Founding Father and President of the United States
Steve Jobs, Co-Founder: Apple Computers
Michael Jordan, Basketball Player
Helen Keller, Author and Political Activist
*Dennis Kimbro, Author: What Makes the Great, Great
*Robert Kiyosaki, Entrepreneur, Author: Rich Dad, Poor Dad
Guy Laliberte, Founder, Cirque du Soleil
Dalai Lama, Spiritual Leader
Abraham Lincoln, 16th President of the United States
Martin Luther King Jr., Civil Rights Leader
Nelson Mandela, President of South Africa
John Maxwell, Author and Leadership Coach
Michelangelo, Renaissance Artist, Architect, Poet, and Engineer
J. P. Morgan, Industrialist
Isaac Newton, Physicists
Earl Nightingale, Motivational Speaker
Norman Vincent Peale, Author
Pablo Picasso, Artist
*Daniel Pink, Author: A Whole New Mind
Plato, Philosopher

Bob Proctor, Author, Speaker and Life Coach
Scott Rigsby, Ironman Triathlete
Shakira Mebarak Ripoll, Colombian Musician, Philanthropist
Tony Robbins, Author, Speaker, and Life Coach
John Rockefeller, American Industrialist
*Anita Roddick, Founder: The Body Shop
Eleanor Roosevelt, Inspirational First Lady of the United States
William Rosenberg, Founder, Dunkin' Donuts
Joane (J.K.) Rowling, Author of Harry Potter Series
Wilma Rudolph, Olympic Gold Medalist
Rumi, Poet and Theologian
William Shakespeare, Renaissance Actor and Author
Mimi Silbert, Founder, Delancey Street Foundation
Will Smith, Actor
W. Clement Stone, Billionaire Businessman and Author
Mother Theresa, Philanthropist
Dave Thomas, Founder, Wendy's
Eckhart Tolle, Author and Life Coach
*Brian Tracy, Author and Life Coach
Donald Trump, Businessman and Author
Ted Turner, Businessman and Author
Desmond Tutu, Political Activist
Mark Twain, Author and Speaker
Lao Tzu, Social Philosopher
Voltaire, Enlightenment Philosopher and Author
Nick Vujicic, Motivational Speaker
*Denis Waitley, Author and Life Coach
George Washington Carver, Scientist, Inventor and Educator
Jerry Weintraub, Hollywood Producer
Oprah Winfrey, Billionaire Talk Show Host
John Wooden, College Basketball Coach
Zhang Xin, Self-Made Female Billionaire, China
*Zig Ziglar, Author and Speaker

* These individuals were personally interviewed by our partner, Mitch Schlimer on the nationally acclaimed radio show, *Let's Talk Business*, now called *7Mindsets Radio* and broadcast weekly on WREK Atlanta 91.1 FM and streamed over the internet.

Appendix B:
Reference Books

Wally Amos, *The Power in You,* (New York: Dutton Adult)

Andy Andrews, *The Butterfly Effect: How Your Life Matters,* (Illinois: Simple Truths, LLC)

Andy Andrews *Mastering the Seven Decisions: That Determine Personal Success,* (Tennessee: Thomas Nelson Publishers)

Janet Bray Attwood and Chris Attwood, *The Passion Test: The Effortless Path to Discovering Your Destiny,* (Iowa: 1st World Publishing)

Doug Bench, *Revolutionize Your Brain,* (Florida: Doug Bench Enterprises)

Richard Branson, *Business Stripped Bare: Adventures of a Global Entrepreneur,* (London: Penguin Books, Ltd.)

Richard Brodie, *Virus of the Mind: The New Science of the Meme,* (California: Hay House)

Brendon Bruchard, *Life's Golden Ticket: An Inspirational Novel,* (New York: HarperCollins)

Marcus Buckingham and Donald O. Clifton *Now Discover Your Strengths,* (New York: Simon & Schuster)

Bob Burg and John David Mann, *The Go-Giver: A Little Story About a Powerful Business Idea,* (London: Penguin Books, Ltd.)

Jack Canfield and Kent Healy, *The Success Principles for Teens: How to Get From Where You Are to Where You Want to Be,* (Florida: Health Communications, Inc.)

Jack Canfield and Janet Switzer, *The Success Principles: How to Get from Where You Are to Where You Want to Be,* (New York, HarperCollins Publishers)

Jack Canfield and Mark Victor Hansen, *The Aladdin Factor,* (New York: Berkley Publishing)

Dale Carnegie, *How to Win Friends and Influence People,* (New York: Simon & Schuster)

Deepak Chopra, *The Seven Spiritual Laws of Success: A Pocketbook Guide to Fulfilling Your Dreams (One Hour Wisdom),* (California: Amber-Allen Publishing and New World Library)

Carol Christen and Richard N. Bolles, *What Color is Your Parachute for Teens: Discovering Yourself, Defining Your Future*, (California: Berkeley Press)

Bill Clinton, *Giving: How Each of Us Can Change the World,* (Canada: Random House)

Paulo Coelho, *The Alchemist,* (New York: HarperCollins)

Jim Collins, *Good to Great: Why Some Companies Make the Leap ... and Others Don't,* (New York: HarperCollins)

Geoff Colvin, *Talent is Overrated: What Really Separates World-Class Performers from Everybody Else,* (New York: Penguin Group)

Stephen Covey, *The 7 Habits of Highly Effective People (New York: Free Press)*

Fred DeLuca and John P. Hays, *Start Small Finish Big: 15 Key Lessons to Start—and Run—Your Own Business,* (New York: Warner Business Books)

Dr. John Demartini, *The Gratitude Effect: The Inner Power Series* (TruMedia Group)

Carol Dweck, *Mindset: The New Psychology of Success*, (New York: Ballentine)

Hale Dwoskin and Jack Canfield, *The Sedona Method: Your Key to Lasting Happiness, Success, Peace and Emotional Well-Being,* (Arizona: Sedona Press)

Dr. Wayne Dyer, *Excuses Begone!: How to Change Lifelong Self Defeating Thinking Habits*, (California: Hayhouse)

Dr. Wayne Dyer, *The Power of Intention*, (California: Hay House)

Ralph Waldo Emerson, *Self Reliance: The Wisdom of Ralph Waldo Emerson as Inspiration of Daily Living,* (New York: Bell Tower)

Mark Forstater, *The Spiritual Teaching of Marcus Aurelius*, (New York: HarperCollins)

Marshall Frady, *Martin Luther King, Jr.: A Life*, (New York: Viking Penguin)

Victor Frankl, *Man's Search for Meaning*, (Massachusetts: Beacon Press)

Neal Gabler, *Walt Disney: The Triumph of American Imagination,* (New York: Alfred Knopf)

Howard Gardner, *Frames of Mind: The Theory of Multiple Intelligences*, (Pennsylvania: Perseus Books)

Michael J. Gelb, *How to Think Like Leonardo daVinci*, (New York: Dell Publishing)

Malcolm Gladwell, *Outliers: The Story of Success*, (New York: Little, Brown and Company)

Shakti Gawain, *Creative Visualization: use the Power of Imagination to Create What You Want in Your Life*, (California, Nataraj Publishing)

Shakti Gawain, *Marianne Williamson, and Mother Theresa, For the Love of God*, (California: Nataraj Publishing Company)

Mark Victor Hansen, *The Richest Kids in America: How They Earn It, How They Spend It, How You Can Too*, (California: Hansen House)

Keith Harrell, *Attitude is Everything Rev Ed: 10 Life-Changing Steps to Turning Attitude into Action*, (New York: HaperCollins)

Daren Hardy, *The Compound Effect: Multiplying Your Success, One Simple Step at a Time*, (Texas: Success Books)

Dr. David R. Hawkins, *Power vs. Force: The Hidden Determinant of Human Behavior*, (California: Hayhouse)

Tony Hsieh, *Delivering Happiness: A Path to Profits, Passion, and Purpose*, (New York: Business Plus)

Napoleon Hill, *Think and Grow Rich*, (New York: Plume)

Napoleon Hill and W. Clement Stone, *Success through a Positive Mental Attitude*, (New York: Simon & Schuster)

Walter Isaacson, *Albert Einstein: His Life and Universe*, (New York: Simon and Shuster)

Susan Jeffers Ph.D., *Feel the Fear... and Do It Anyway*, (New York: Ballentine)

Paul Johnson, *Churchill*, (New York: Viking)

Willie Jolley, *It Only Takes a Minute to Change Your Life*, (New York: St. Martin's Press)

Michael Jordan and Mark Vancil, *I Can't Accept Not Trying: Michael Jordan on the Pursuit of Excellence*, (California: Harper)

Helen Keller, *The Story of My Life*, (New York: Doubleday)

Dennis Kimbro, *Think and Grow Rich: A Black Choice*, (New York: Fawcett Books)

Dennis Kimbro , *What Makes the Great Great*, (New York: Main Street Books)

Martin Luther King, Jr., *The Autobiography of Martin Luther King, Jr., Ed. Clayborne Carson*, (New York: Warner Books, Inc.)

Charles G. Koch, *The Science of Success: How Market-Based Management Built the World's Largest Private Company* (New Jersey: John Wiley & Sons)

Jennifer Kushell, *Secrets of the Young and Successful*, (Princeton Review)

Robert Kiyosaki, *Rich Dad Poor Dad: What The Rich Teach Their Kids About Money –That The Poor And Middle Class Do Not!* (:TechPress)

H.H.Dalai Lama, *The Art of Happiness*, (New York: Riverhead Books)

Ellen J. Langer, *Mindfulness*, (Pennsylvania: Perseus Books Group)

Bruce H. Lipton, Ph.D., *The Biology of Belief: Unleashing the Power of Consciousness, Matter, & Miracles*, (California: Hay House)

Nelson Mandela, *Long Walk to Freedom: The Autobiography of Nelson Mandela*, (New York: Back Bay Books)

John Maxwell, *Talent is Never Enough: Discover the Choices that Will Take You Beyond Your Talent*, (Tennessee: Thomas Nelson)

John Maxwell, *The 21 Irrefutable Laws of Leadership*, (Tennessee: Thomas Nelson)

George McGovern, *Abraham Lincoln,* (New York: Times Books)

Jay McGraw, *Life Strategies for Teens,* (New York: Fireside)

Dr. Phil McGraw, *Life Strategies: Doing what Works, Doing What Matters*, (New York: Hyperion)

James M. McPherson, *Abraham Lincoln and the 2nd American Revolution,* (New York: Oxford University Press)

Dan Millman, *The Way of the Peaceful Warrior: A Book That Changes Lives,* (H.J. Kramer)

Stephen Mitchell, *The Tao Te Ching: A New English Version,* New York: HarperCollins

Greg Mortenson *Three Cups of Tea,* (New York: Penguin Books)

Joseph Murphy, *The Power of Your Subconscious Mind,* (New York: Bantam)

Lisa Nichols, *No Matter What!: 9 Steps to Living the Life You Love*, (New York: Hachette Book Group)

Dr. Norman Vincent Peale, *The Power of Positive Thinking*, (New York: Fireside)

M. Scott Peck, M.D., *The Road Less Traveled: A New Psychology of Love, Traditional Values and Spiritual Growth,* (New York: Touchstone)

Daniel Pink, *Drive: The Surprising Truth About What Motivates Us,* (New York: Riverhead Books)

Daniel Pink, *A Whole New Mind : Why Right-Brainers Will Rule the Future,* (New York: Berkley Publishing)

Steven Pinker, *The Stuff of Thought: Language As a Window into Human Nature*, (New York: Penguin Publishing)

James Redfield, *The Celestine Prophecy*, (New York: Warner Books)

Scott Rigsby, *Unthinkable,* (Illinois: Tyndale House)

Alexandra Robbins and Ab Wilner, *Quarterlife Crisis: The Unique Challenges of Life in Your Twenties,* (New York, Jeremy P Tarcher/Putnam)

Anthony Robbins, *Awaken the Giant Within: How to Take Immediate Control of Your Mental, Emotional, Physical and Financial Destiny!*, (New York: Free Press)

Anthony Robbins, *Unlimited Power: The New Science of Personal Achievement*, (New York: Free Press)

Ken Robinson, Ph.D., *The Element: How Finding Your Passion Changes Everything*, (New York: Penguin Publishing)

Jim Rohn, *Three Keys to Greatness for Teenagers*, (audible edition: made for Success, Inc.)

Jim Rohn, *The Art of Exceptional Living,* (Illinois: Nightingale-Conant)

Miguel Ruiz, *The Four Agreements: A Practical Guide to Personal Freedom* (California: Amber-Allen Publ)

SQuire Rushnell, *When GOD Winks: How the Power of Coincidence Guides Your Life,* (New York: Atria Books)

Martin Seligman, *Authentic Happiness: Using the New Positive Psychology to Realize Your Potential for Deep Fulfillment*, (Boston: Nicholas Brealey)

Martin E.P. Seligman, Ph.D., *Learned Optimism: How to Change Your Mind and Your Life*, (New York: Simon & Schuster)

Marci Shimoff, *Happy for No Reason: 7 Steps to Being Happy from the Inside Out*, (New York: Free Press)

Florence Scovel Shinn, *The Game of Life and How to Play It*, (Tribeca Books)

Sam Smith, *The Jordan Rules*, (New York: Pocket Books)

Mother Teresa and Brian Kolodiejchuk, *Come be My Light*, (New York: Random House)

Eckhart Tolle, *The Power of Now*, (Canada: Namaste Publishing)

Eckhart Tolle, *A New Earth*, (New York: Penguin Publishing)

W. Clement Stone and Michael Ritt, *Believe and Achieve: W. Clement Stone's 17 Principles of Success*, (Pennsylvania: Executive Books)

Lao Tzu and Brian Brown Walker, *The Tao Te Ching Lao Tzu*, (New York: St. Martin's Press)

Brian Tracy, *Maximum Achievement: Strategies and Skills that Will Unlock Your Hidden Power to Succeed*, (New York: Fireside)

Christiane Turner, *Quantum NLP : From Personal to Global Transformation*, (New York: Gilden Media)

Neale Donald Walsch, *Conversations with God*, (New York: Penguin Publishing)

Rick Warren, *The Purpose Driven Life: What on Earth am I Here For?*, (Michigan: Zondervan)

Liz Wiseman and Greg McKeown, *Multipliers: How the Best Leaders Make Everyone Smarter*, (New York: HarperCollins)

Steve Young, *Great Failures of the Extremely Successful: Mistake, Adversity, Failure and other Stepping Stones to Success*, (California: Tallfellow Press)

Muhammad Yunus, *Banker to the Poor: Micro-Lending and the Battle Against Poverty*, (New York: Public Affairs)

"The principles instituted by The 7 Mindsets represent a phenomenal construction that changed my perception and elevated my potential to set and achieve my goals in a manner that was never exposed to me before. Their power lies in their capability to alter the negative evaluation of one's personal attributes into progressive outlooks that fundamentally help in self-improvement, and subsequently, in communal development. I truly believe that if those 7 Mindsets were introduced to the youth here in the United Arab Emirates, the outcome will be pleasantly rewarding."

Fatma Alshowab
Graduate Student, United Arab Emirates

"An extreme amplification of happiness, success, motivation and service came to my life after being exposed to the 7 Mindsets. These mindsets are so clear and efficient that making them a lifestyle is extremely easy and helpful."

Karen Carvajalino Martinez
Student, Colombia

"The 7 Mindsets have opened my mind and thousands of doors that will lead to success in my life. They have opened my eyes and helped me to know that I will reach my fullest potential. I wish so much that many more students from the Dominican Republic could share my experience."

Carla Rodriguez Dajer
Student, Dominican Republic

"The 7 Mindsets are based on principles that are a critical tool to helping a person unlock mental barriers that keep the majority of people from experiencing a fulfilled, successful life. Since my exposure to the 7 Mindsets, I have used them personally to inspire new ideas and solidify my attitude to succeed professionally. I also use them to inspire and encourage youth. Through great stories and the scientific research to back up the results, the 7 Mindsets will awaken the hope to achieve your personal definition of success!"

Lazarus Bruner Jr.
Educator/Entrepreneur

"The 7 Mindsets showed me a different way to see and experience life, especially a different way to treat people and live my passion."

Stephanie Carvajalino Martinez
Student, Colombia

"I have always strived to reach my full potential; however, it was not until I dug deep into the 7 Mindsets that I realized my potential is unlimited! I now truly believe. Everything is Possible when one holds a positive mindset. I have been inspired not only to dream bigger than ever before, but to take action to achieve my biggest dreams."

Stephanie Johnston
Student, Fargo ND

"I have seen the radical and positive change among youth while living the 7 Mindsets. Learning them is truly a life changing experience. They are a practical guide to positive personal challenges for all of us with a global vision and positive change."

Jorge Olmos
Educator, Mexico City, Mexico

"The mindsets are powerful and can change the way you see yourself and how you go through your life... Go for it!!!! EVERYTHING IS POSSIBLE!!! THE TIME IS NOW!!!"

Lisa Hess
Educator, Florida

"The 7 Mindsets have proved to me that I can live my dreams; that they become very realistic once you define them and start taking the necessary steps. I believe their greatest power is in inspiring young people from all over the world to live better lives and work together to build a better society and planet!"

Itzel Polin
Student, Mexico City, Mexico

"Not just a set of ideas, but a way of living. The 7 Mindsets teach you how to live a happier and more successful life. It taught me happiness is not the destination, it's the journey."

George Moore
Student, London, England